TEACHER'S HANDBOOK OF ENGLISH

ANMOL PUBLICATIONS PVT. LTD.
H.O.: 4374/4B, Ansari Road, Darya Ganj
New Delhi-110 002 (India)
Ph.: 23278000, 23261597
B.O.: 1015, Ist Main Road, BSK IIIrd Stage
IIIrd Phase, IIIrd Block
Bangalore - 560 085 (Karnataka)
Ph: 080-41723429, Tel/Fax: 080-2672 3604
Visit us at: www.anmolpublications.com

Teacher's Handbook of English

First Published, 2007

PRINTED IN INDIA

Printed at Mehra Offset Press, Delhi.

TEACHER'S HANDBOOK OF ENGLISH

M.H. Syed

ANMOL PUBLICATIONS PVT. LTD.
NEW DELHI - 110 002 (INDIA)

CONTENTS

Preface ix

1. **Introduction** 1
Theory of Scientific Learning • Education and Guidance • Common Theory • The Effects • Theory of Psychology • Various Languages

2. **Art of English Teaching** 27
Theory of Meaning • Philosophical View • The Applicability • The Recital • Paying Attention • The Conversation

3. **Teaching Methods** 45
Different Methods • Direct Approach • Structure and Pattern • The Variations • Grammar vs Translation Method

4. **Aims of Teaching English** 59
Behavioural Objectives • Learning Objectives • The Variations • Various Goals • Resultant Objectives • Various Plans • The Interrelation • Perceiving the Aims

5. Teaching Aids 89

Modern Devices • The Division • The Illustration • Multi-Dimensional Aids • Definition and Significance • The Importance

6. Special Difficulties in English Teaching 123

Significance of Mother Tongue • A Foreign Language • Input and Output System • Complications Ahead • Complications in the System • Procedure of Assessment • Functions of the Guardian • Achievements • Ability of a Teacher • Research Necessity

7. Place of English in Education 135

Elite Language • Importance of English • Role of Britishers • Initial Phase • Complications in Language Learning • Three-Language Scheme • School Syllabus

8. Significance of Textbooks 153

Collaborative Publication • Functions of a Guide • Complication in Marketing • Fundamental Requirements • Contribution of Private Publishers • Contribution of Central Government • Contribution of State Governments • Double Efforts

9. Significance of Writing 197

Writing Counsel • The Progress • The Illustration • Importance of Script • Language Items

10. Significance of Reading 211

Different Kinds • Audible Reading • Mock Reading • Limited and Wide Reading

• Various Kinds • Habitual Growth • The Meaning • The Importance • The Application

11. Test of Ability 229

Various Aspects • Ideal Plan • Different Growth Models • The Assimilation-oriented Test • Goal-oriented Test • Classical Goal-oriented Test

12. Beyond Teaching and Learning 237

Plan for Literacy • Collaborative Plan • Acquiring Knowledge • Schemes for Slow Learners • Main Objectives • Gainful Work • Special Profit • The Evaluation • Improvement and Solution Method • Meaning and History

Bibliography 261

Index 263

PREFACE

Teaching is a noble profession. It involves honour, prestige, knowledge-updated information, money and much more. From primary to higher education, a teacher is looked upon as an ideal for students. Students make all efforts to imitate their teacher in every respect. As for knowledge, students regard teachers as a moving store-house of information and erudition, where every question has an answer.

A teacher (mostly upto 10+2 levels) has to perform a number of duties other than teaching. That's why he or she finds little time to prepare 'lesson plans' and other material to be taught in classroom.

While taking a class, the teacher should seem to be moving in the etherial realm of knowledge. He or she should be well prepared and there should not be even the slightest hint of hesitation or lack of confidence. For this purpose, a thorough preparation is necessary. However, extra-curricular activities do not allow a teacher to make sufficient preparation for classroom teaching.

To overcome the problem, present series of handbooks on every subject has been prepared. It would save time and energy of a teacher, on one hand, and provide sufficient feedback on the concerned subject, in a short time, on the other. Simultaneously, it would instil confidence in teachers to address any query, posed by the students on the topic under discussion or teaching.

This particular book is titled: *Teachers' Handbook of English.*

Hopefully, it would serve busy teachers, to a great extent, in providing them, with a cut-and-dried solution to every problem and all issues, under one cover. For further enhancement and betterment of the endeavour, in future, I solicit and appreciate wise comments and useful suggestions from esteemed readers.

— Editor

One

INTRODUCTION

Being complex social and cultural phenomenon, teaching is not as easy to teach as it appears. While teaching, a teacher has to keep in mind the aims and objectives of his subject, needs, interests of his pupils, the environmental situation suitable for them etc. Success of this profession depends upon good planning and mastery in the subject to be taught. Hence for helping the teacher, some principles have been designed on the basis of general experiences, traditions and researches. These principles provide guidelines to the teacher as to what methods should be adopted in the class-room to increase the teaching efficiency.

A good teacher always wants that his teaching should be effective. He wants that all the students of the class should properly attend, listen to him and try to grasp what he teaches in the class. The principles evolved help the teacher to carry on his routine of teaching efficiently. They provide him guidelines and keep him on the right track. They check him from going astray. They ensure the achievement of the teacher in the process of teaching.

THEORY OF SCIENTIFIC LEARNING

All the psychological principles effect the teaching-learning process considerably. A good teaching always keeps those principles in mind and thus ensures good teaching-learning. Here below are given the implications of the different psychological principles.

a. The teacher motivates the students in the class and that makes everybody interested in the process of teaching-learning. Through motivation, the teacher becomes a source of joy for the learners. When the carriers are interested in the teacher, then they also like his activity of teaching.

b. A good teacher is not always busy- in just finishing the prescribed course of study. He repeats matter and also gives sufficient practice so that it is fully understood by them.

c. Feedback and reinforcement are very important in the process of teaching-learning. If a test is held, the teacher should tell the students about their results as early as possible. Immediate feedback helps them to learn more.

d. The teacher should keep in mind the principle of variety. A good teacher uses different methods of teaching and that keeps the students fully interested in the process of teaching-learning.

e. The principle of rest and recreation changes the attitude of the teacher. So a teacher while teaching takes care of the fact that the students have some rest in between. He also recreates them. All this helps the teacher to teach better and the learner is also able to learn more.

f. A good teacher prepares the students first for his teaching and then only he starts teaching. This is bound to improve teaching-learning.

g. Creative teaching is good. The teacher should teach in such a way as the learners become creative.

h. A sympathetic type of teacher is able to win the hearts of the learners. The teacher should always be cooperative with the students. Let cooperation flow from the teacher first. That will make the whole teaching-learning quite effective.

i. The teacher should not give spoon feeding to the learners. He should arouse their interest and develop in them love for self-learning. This practice reduces the load of work of the teacher. The student is also able to learn really.

j. While teaching a group, the teacher should keep in mind the group behaviour of learners. Then only he will be able to teach well.

Principles of teaching are, undoubtedly effective tools in the hands of a teacher. Only a good teacher is able to put them to right use. The saying a bad workman quarrels with his tools is perfectly true. The different principles of teaching can work wonders in the hands of a good teacher. The teachers under training are, therefore advised to keep the principles of teaching in mind while teaching. It is bound to make them better and better teachers in due course of time.

The Oxford Dictionary defines Maxim as a general truth drawn from science of experience. Over the years various educationists have given numerous rules of conduct for teaching which may be called maxims. These maxims are the true facts found out by the teacher on the basis of experience. They are of universal significance and are trustworthy. Every teacher is expected to familiarise himself with the time honoured maxims of teaching. The knowledge of different maxims help the teacher to proceed systematically. It also smoothens his way of teaching especially at the early stages of teaching.

The different maxims of teaching are briefly explained below. The teacher should always proceed keeping them in view:

Known to Unknown: This maxim is based on the assumption that the student knows something. We are to increase his knowledge and widen his outlook. We have to interpret all new knowledge in terms of old. It is said that old knowledge serves as a hook on which the new one can be hung. Known is trustworthy and unknown cannot be trusted.

So while teaching we should proceed from known and go towards unknown. For example, while teaching any lesson, the teacher can link the previous experiences of the child with the new lesson that is to be taught.

Suppose the teacher is teaching English to the children and he is to teach the word 'book.' He reminds them the Hindi word *'Pustak'* which they already know and then he tells them that in English we say 'book'. This way of teaching helps the learners to understand things fully.

Simple to Complex: Class-room teaching is formal where the teacher tries to teach and the students try to learn things. In this process of teaching-learning, the teacher should see that simple things are presented first to the students- That way they will start taking interest.

Once they become interested, then gradually complex type of things can also be learnt by them. By learning simple things, they feel encouraged and the also gain confidence. On that basis, they become further receptive to the complex matter. On the other hand, if complex type of things are presented to the learner first he becomes upset, feels bored and finds himself in a challenging situation for which he is not yet ready being immature and unripe.

Simplicity or complexity of the subject matter should be determined according to the viewpoint of the learners. Gradually more difficult items of learning may be presented to the students. It will smoothen teaching being done by the teacher and make learning convenient and interesting for the students.

For example, while teaching sentences of English simple sentences should be taught first and complex type of sentences may be taken afterwards.

Concrete to Abstract: Concrete things are solid things and they can be visualised. But abstract things are only imaginative things. So it is rather difficult to teach the children about abstract things. The students are likely to forget them soon. On the other hand, if we teach the students with the help of concrete objects, they will never forget the subject matter. *Froebel* said, "Our lesson ought to start in the concrete and end in the abstract."

For example, when we teach counting to the students we should first take the help of concrete objects like, beads, stones etc. and then proceed to digits and numbers. The stars, the moon, the sun etc. being concrete should be taught first whereas the abstract things like plants, satellites etc. should be taught afterwards.

Analysis to Synthesis: Analysis means breaking a problem into its convenient parts while synthesis means grouping of these separated parts into one complete whole. A complex problem can be made simple and easy by dividing into units.

"Analysis is the approach for understanding and synthesis is for fixation." Analysis of a sentence is taught to the students, that helps the students to understand the different parts of a sentence. Later on, synthesis of sentences should be taught.

Particular to General: While teaching, the teacher should first of all take particular statements and then on the basis of those particular cases, generalisation should be made. Suppose the teacher is teaching present continuous tense while teaching a English, he should first of all give a few examples and then on the basis of those make them generalize that this tense is used to denote an action that is going on at the time of speaking.

Empirical to Rational: Empirical knowledge is based on observation and first hand experience. It is particular, concrete and simple. We can see, feel and experience it. On the other hand, rational is based on our arguments and explanation. The stage of arguments is the last whereas seeing things or feeling them is the first stage. Empirical is less general statements whereas rational is more general statements. So the safe approach in teaching is that we should proceed from empirical to rational. It is less mental maturity to more mental maturity.

Induction to Deduction: Induction means drawing a conclusion from a set of examples whereas deduction is its opposite. The teacher should proceed from induction to deduction. For example, in English while teaching conversion of active voice into passive voice. 'The teacher should first convert a few sentences of active into the passive voice and on the basis of those conclude the general rule for conversation of active voice into passive voice.

Psychological to Logical: While teaching, the teacher should first keep in mind the interest, aptitudes, capacities, development level etc. of the children during selection of subject matter and then on to its logical arrangement.

In teaching English, the structures are selected as per needs and requirements of the students and then arranged in a logical way. The psychological appeal of the thing is more important at the early stages. Then the logic behind it should be seen.

Actual to Representative: For teaching excellently, actual objects should be shown to the children as far as possible. It gives them concrete learning which is more desirable. The learners are able to retain it in their minds for quite a long time. Specially in the lower classes first hand information to the students impresses them a good deal. Representative things in the form of pictures, models etc. should be used for the grown ups or the seniors who are already familiar with the actual objects.

For example, the teacher should show the elephant, the

camel, the horse, the railway station, the post office etc. and thereby he should make them understand about these things. The representative of these things in the form of pictures or models may be used at later stages.

Near to A far: Every child is able to learn well in the surroundings to which he belongs. So the child should be acquainted fully with his immediate environment. Gradually he may be taught about those things which are a far from his immediate environment. This principle, if kept in view ill smoothen the teaching-learning process considerably. Thus the child should be taught the home, followed by the street, the bazar, the school and then the distant environment of the city to which he belongs.

In the same way acquaintance with the city should lead to acquaintance with the Tehsil- the District, the Division, the State and then the Country as a whole. This type of teaching will be incremental and will be step by step learning. The textbook writer who writes books for the small children should also place the different chapters in his book keeping in view of this principle. Then only his book will stand better chances of approval by all concerned.

Whole to Part: In teaching, the teacher should try to acquaint the child with the whole lesson first and then the different portions of it may be analysed and studied intensively This principle holds good while teaching a thing to the small children. At the early stages, the child loves to speak full sentences because in daily life situations, full sentences are used. The child should be given a full sentence. Then he may have full familiarity with the different words contained in that sentence. Later he may have the knowledge of words. Then he will have the knowledge of different letters forming the words.

Suppose a poem is to be taught to the students. They should be acquainted with the full poem first. Gradually they may be asked to grasp the poem stanza by stanza. In the case of average students, their first attempt may be on a full stanza, taking it as a whole and then to the different lines contained in the stanza as parts. It will help the teacher to teach better and the learners to learn things conveniently.

Definite to Indefinite: In teaching, definite things should be taught first because the learner can easily have faith in them. Gradually he should be given the knowledge of indefinite things. Definite things, definite rules of grammar help the learner to have good knowledge. Gradually he can be taught about indefinite things.

The above given maxims are only hints and guidelines for the teacher especially at the initial stages. He may use them if he finds some of them useful in his teaching situations. In some situations of class-room teaching, he may not use them if he feels so. The teacher should keep the maxims in his hand and he himself should remain their master. Then only the different maxims will remain tools and yield better results.

EDUCATION AND GUIDANCE

Teaching learning of a language is a matter of practice. The language teacher can teach the language any way he likes. But the knowledge and application of certain principles help him to teach the same language effectively. While teaching, the teacher must keep in mind the learner, his capability and capacity to learn and above all his environment of learning. Some teachers knowingly use difficult words of English while teaching. They forget the mental ability and the grasping capacity of the learners. That type of teaching is not good. Effective teaching of a language is based on certain principles. Some of the basic principles for teaching the language effectively are explained below:

Imitation: Learning of any language is based on the principle of imitation. In fact, imitation is natural to man. From childhood, language is best learnt through imitation. It is especially true in the case of small children. Whatever they see all around them, they mutate those things in the same way. Sometimes even the wrong habits of the teacher are carried on by the small children.

If a teacher has poor pronunciation, his students at the early stages of learning the language will pick up the same poor standard of pronunciation from him. The bad handwriting of the teacher may also have adverse effect on the learners. It has been seen that if some teacher is in the habit of writing with left hand, the students under his charge also acquire that habit of writing with left hand.

So the teacher who is given the charge of teaching the small children must be good through and through. He should have a model type of pronunciation. His handwriting should be very good. He must possess good habits. All this will have very good impact on the growing personalities of the small children. It is, therefore, very strongly recommended that really good teachers should be recruited for teaching the small children in the schools.

Practice and Drill: Learning of language is a habit formation process. Habits are formed through repetition. Continuous practice and drill work are needed for it. All aspects of language learning i.e. listening, speaking, reading and writing can be acquired after a lot of practice. They should learn to use the language correctly though they may not know the rules of grammar. Robert Lado says, "To know the language is to use its patterns of construction with appropriate vocabulary at normal speed for communication."

Practice makes a man perfect. Learning a language is more a matter of skill rather than of knowledge. Robert Lado rightly says, "The student must be engaged in practice most of the learning time. This principle has a psychological justification since other things being equal, the quantity and permanence of learning are in direct proportion to the amount of practice." In this regard, Fries recommended eighty four percent of time be devoted to practice and fifteen per cent time be utilized for explanation and commentary.

Thompson and Wyatt write in their book The Teaching of English in India'. "The power of expression in a language is a matter of skill rather than of merely meanings or rules." In the learning of a language the students require a lot of practice and drill work.

Only then they will be able to learn it properly. Language learning or teaching is not a knowledge subject, it is rather a skill subject like swimming, dancing painting etc. So the learner will have to repeat and revise things in order to have mastery over the language. The various skills of language learning i.e. listening, speaking, reading and writing will be properly- learnt through practice and drill work.

Otto Jesperson says, "He who gets the tip of his finger dipped in the water three times in twenty weeks will never lean, how to swim." There is need of continuous practice for acquisition of every skill.

Oral Approach: Language is more connected with ears and tongue than with eyes. So in the teaching of English, oral work should be given topmost priority. If a students is good at spoken language, he will automatically be good in reading and writing of the language. Moreover, whatever is learnt orally is remembered better. So due emphasis should be laid on this aspect of the language.

Selection and Gradation: In the teaching of a language, selection and gradation of language items are very important. Selection may be done by the teacher, in respect of grammatical items, vocabulary and structures. Selection and gradation should involve frequency, teachability, range of applicability, usefulness etc.

Selection: The selection of language items should be based on the following principles:

1. Frequency of language items-its occurrence.
2. Range of applicability i.e. in how many contexts it is applicable.
3. Coverage-a word conveying a number of meanings e.g. meals stand for dinner, breakfast etc.
4. Availability-the items which can be conveniently taught e.g. actual objects available in the class-room like table, chair, chalk etc.
5. Teachability-items which are easy from teaching point of view.
6. Learnability-items which are easy for the students to learn should be taken up first.

Gradation: Gradation means putting the language items in order of presentation. Thus simple items having more utility and better teachability will be taken care of. Gradation involves grouping and sequence. The basic principle of grading according to W.R. Lee is: "Teach first there sentences structures the use of which can be made clear by means of visible actions in the class room.

(a) Grouping

(i) Group according to the sound e.g. pay, bat, say, sat etc. This is called phonetic grouping.

(ii) Grouping according to words used in the same situation e.g. words connected with post office-post master, postman, dak, letters, it is called lexical grouping.

(iii) Patterns of sentences which are similar should be taught together e.g., This is, that is my book, your book etc. called grammatical grouping should be taught together.

(iv) Semantic grouping words that convey similar

meanings are grouped together e.g. shelter, hut, house, tent etc.

(v) Structure grouping-bow the selected items fit with each other sounds into words, words into phrases. phrases into sentences and sentences into contexts.

(b) Sequence-What comes after what.

(i) Lexical sequence-which words follow which e.g. sit, stand, come, go.

(ii) Grammatical Sequence-means which structure follows which.

S.V.O. For example,

I am throwing a ball.

I am throwing a ball to you.

(iii) Semantic sequence-Every word has a number of meanings. They are put in order and are taught at different occasions e.g., the word 'there'

(a) The pen is there. (Place)

(b) There are many pens. (Introduction)

Motivation or Interest: Motivation or interest is of great importance in the teaching-learning process. Language is learnt quickly if interest is created in it. So the language teacher should make use of different types of aids for this purpose. Some interesting methods like activity method, playway method can also be used. Thus the learners remain captivated and learn things very actively They are also able to retain those things in their minds for a longer time.

The general poor standard of students in English is due to the lack of interest. Many students learn English half-heartedly. They consider it a necessary evil. The teachers themselves are seen criticising English in their class rooms. How can there be good teaching-learning of English when both the teacher and the taught lack interest? The teacher who cannot make his teaching interesting, should better quit the teaching profession. He should be able to deal with the solutions in such a way that the learners should become interested both in their teacher and the subject matter.

Natural Way of Teaching-Learning: Natural process of learning the language should be followed. Listening and speaking should precede reading and writing. The teacher should lay more emphasis on the first two aspect i.e., listening and speaking. Then the learners will automatically be good at reading and writing of the language.

Some people are of the opinion that listening to some other language, unless mother tongue is fully learnt, is dangerous. But it is not true. In this regard, *Dr. Penfield* rightly says, "A child who hears three languages instead of one, early enough learns the units of all the three without added efforts and without confusion." *Jesperson* says "The very first lesson in a foreign language ought to be devoted to initiating the pupil into the world of sounds."

Language should be Learnt in Context and Situation: Language is taught so that the learners are able to make use of it in their day-to-day life situations. Different language items-say vocabulary structures etc. should be dealt with in the context of some appropriate situations so that the learner may find them very near to life. In the words of *Eugene A. Nida* "Language learning means plunging headlong into a series of completely different experiences. It means exposing oneself to situations where the use of language is required." It is, therefore, very essential that vocabulary items should be learnt in the context of a sentence or sentences and the sentences should be learnt in situations. Only then teaching-learning will be more effective and meaningful.

Adoption of Multiple Line of Approach: While teaching a foreign language, the multiple line of approach should be followed as it helps the learners and the teacher in many ways. Suppose a class is to be taught an essay on 'Diwali'. First of all, there should be oral work and after that the students may be asked to write a few sentences on that topic in their note books. Spelling practice is given out of the same topic. While doing translation, sentences on the topic 'Diwali' be given. Thus our approach to language would be many sided. By correlating the different aspects of the language, we can certainly make the learning of language easy, interesting and useful.

Balanced Approach: While teaching the language, the teacher should see that the different aspects of it are fully taken care of listening, speaking, reading and writing should be equally emphasized. Each aspect has its own importance. It is not proper if a teacher -teaches grammar and ignores other things. In the same way, emphasis on written work alone does not help much.

In this regard *Palmer* says, "The principle of proportion does not necessarily imply quality of treatment nor even a fixed standard of ratio; it simply means that all items in the whole range of subjects and aspects must receive an appropriate degree of attention so that the student's knowledge of them may ultimately form a harmonious whole."

There should be proper co-ordination in teaching different aspects of the foreign language. Thus in teaching a prose lesson, grammar aspect may be discussed side by side. While doing written composition, oral aspect should also be covered. Thus a sort of balance between the different aspects of language should be maintained.

Swami Vivekananda says, "Arise, awake and stop not till the goal is achieved. " A good teacher is ever in search of new principles of teaching. He is always keen to make use of them in his teaching. Thus his aim is to make his teaching better and better. He works for the satisfaction of his inner wish of having excellence in teaching. He, therefore, finds inspiration in every type of situation and then he works with full zeal and vigour and thus ensures better outcomes of his teaching. He works for excellence oriented education and having applied the different principles, he is able to have quality based education.

COMMON THEORY

A few principles of teaching which are of general nature are explained below:

Principle of Definite Objectives: While teaching anything, the teacher should first of all fix up some objectives. Then he can select the material, use the appropriate methods and then ultimately ensure the attainment of those objectives. In the absence of definite objectives teaching may not remain purposeful activity. The learners may also deviate and may fail to achieve anything solid.

Objectives may vary from subject to subject and from time to time. Behind teaching English, the objectives usually are listening, speaking reading and writing. But at present in free India, the objective of reading for comprehension is being emphasized. So in teaching, the objectives should be fixed and then efforts be made to achieve them.

Principle of Model Presentation: The teacher who presents the material while teaching should see that his presentation is really a model one in every way. The personality of the teacher, his behaviour actions etc. should be model. The learners imitate the teacher to the maximum. So the teacher should present all excellences of life in him which he ultimately wants the learners to acquire in life. The pronunciation of the language that he uses for teaching should be reasonably good. Through his behaviour he should reflect regularity punctuality, honesty, truth, sincerity etc. Then only he will be able to make his learners reach the goals of ideal life. That way only his teaching will come out to be worthwhile and profit yielding for the humanity.

Principle of Selection of Material: In teaching whatever material is to be presented by the teacher should be well selected. It should be in accordance with the aims and objectives of teaching. It should also be according to the likings and the mental level of the learners. Then only it will be digested by the students properly. The right selection of material will result into proper teaching and hence desired results.

Suppose the teacher wants to teach composition. For this he selects topics keeping the syllabus in view the mental level of the learners, their teachability, their learnability etc. This type of material will make the teaching efficient.

Principle of Gradation: The material which is selected should be graded properly. By gradation we mean which item will come at serial No. 1, which item after that end which item at the end. While grading the material, easy and simple things will come first and difficult and complicated things will occur afterwards. Thus placement of material in graded form will make teaching-learning process more effective.

Suppose the teacher has selected 10 essays of English for teaching some class. By gradation these essays will be numbered as 1, 2, 3 etc. which means that essay No. 1 will be taught first and essay No. 2 will come afterwards.

Principle of Activity: The traditional methods of filling up the minds of the children with a lot of information are useless now. The learners sitting passive in the class are not considered good students. Teaching-learning is a bipolar process. Both the teacher and the students should remain active. The more the activity of the children, the better is the teaching-learning process.

Every subject every-topic within a subject can be taught through activity method. An intelligent teacher tries to involve the maximum number of students in his teaching. That makes guaranteed learning by the students. Moreover, the students do not feel any type of lethargy or boredom.

Principle of Correlation: Good teaching makes the students feel everything for better life. The learner in the class-room feels as if he is being prepared for better life. A good teacher tries to correlate his teaching with life. He also tries to correlate one subject with various other subjects which the student is expected to study.

According to *John Dewey* "Education and life are two different names for the same phenomenon. Education which does not prepare the student for life is meaningless. Suppose the teacher is teaching arithmetic to the students, he should enable the students to apply that knowledge in his day to day life situations. While making purchases in the market the student can apply the knowledge of mathematics and thus he feels happy and satisfied.

The teacher of English should also teach English in such a way so that the student feels that he is becoming a better social being by the study of this subject. He should be enabled to speak English with his parents, relatives, teachers or friends. He should also be able to listen to TV Programmes telecast in English. It will give him a lot of confidence.

While teaching one subject the teacher should try to correlate that subject with some other subject which the student studies. It will make his whole studies interesting for him. The child may also get the sort of feeling that the different subjects are preparing him for better life.

Principle of Child Centredness: Teaching should be made child centred as far as possible and it should not be allowed to remain teacher centred as it has been so far. By child centredness we mean interest and liking of the student should be given priority while teaching.

No subject matter should be made meaningful for the child. It should be taught to the child as per his liking and in no case it should be thrust upon him. Thus the child who is not interested in studies should not be compelled to study. He should first of all be mentally prepared for studies. Then only any teaching done for him will be of any use.

Suppose the child wants to study English. In that case teacher should teach him that subject and not some other subject which the teacher wants to teach. An intelligent teacher is able to deal with this type of situations very wisely. In the above situation, he initiates teaching English to the child as per his desire but gradually he makes the child shift to the other subject which the teacher wants to teach.

Principle of Cooperation: Teaching-learning is a cooperative venture of all concerned. For the best teaching, the teacher, the students, the Head of the institution, the parents and everyone else concerned with it cooperates. Then only there is efficient teaching and good learning by the students. Sometimes the Head of the school does not cooperate with the teachers, the result is poor teaching. Thus, cooperation of the teacher, the taught and the Head of the Institution forms the basis of efficient teaching-learning.

Principle of Planning: The principle of planning is the *sine qua non* of efficient teaching. The teacher comes prepared with everything planned before entering into the class. He tries to foresee the problems and he thinks of their possible solutions. Thus the principle of planning helps him to perform his duty of teaching excellently. A good teacher keeps his planning flexible throughout. He may mould things here or there according to the need and requirements of the learners in different situations.

Principle of Individual Differences: In any group of students, no two individuals are exactly the same. There are always variations as far as likings and dislikings, attitudes and aptitudes are concerned. The teacher teaching the whole group by using one and the same method and dealing with everyone in the same way will fail miserably. A good teacher expects the individual differences among the students. He tries to deal with the students according to their individual differences. He tries to satisfy one and all by using different tactics and strategies of teaching.

THE EFFECTS

General principles of teaching affect the teacher and the learner in many ways which are briefly explained below:

a. In every teaching-learning activity, aims are fixed up. A good teacher always keeps these aims ir. view while teaching. Thus the teacher remains on the right track and he works meaningfully. Both the teacher and the taught are able to make right efforts for the attainment of goals already fixed up.

b. The teacher tries to present the subject matter to the learners in the best possible way. He tries to put up his best before the learners so that they also come out very good as a result thereof.

c. A good teacher selects the material very carefully and then only he presents it before the learners. Surely he keeps in mind certain principles for the selection of material. In this way, the subject matter does not pose any problem to the learners. The teacher is able to handle the selected material, well while teaching. The students are also able to understand the subject matter fully.

d. Gradation of material helps a lot in the process of teaching-learning. So the teacher grades the material after its selection and then only he presents it in the class-room. This makes the teaching-learning process successful.

e. The teacher keeps in mind the principle of variety. He tries to bring in variety in a number of ways so that no student finds teaching-learning a drudgery or boredom.

f. The teacher tries to correlate the subject matter with the different life-situations of the students. Many a time, the teacher correlates the topic with other subjects being taught to the students. It helps the teacher to teach the subject matter effectively and the learners are also able to learn it well.

g. The teacher tries to make his teaching child-centred. He sees everything from learner's point of view. Thus the students find it useful for them and they do not feel any type of imposition on them.

h. The teacher cooperates with the students during the process of teaching-learning. Then naturally all students cooperate fully with the teacher. This creates healthy environment and makes teaching-learning more effective.

i. The teacher always plans the lesson before teaching. Naturally, thus his teaching will be systematic and will be liked by all concerned with it. Systematic teaching helps in better learning by the students.

j. When the teacher knows that no two students are of the same type in liking, interest, attitude etc., he tries to teach in such a way that majority of them are benefited. He becomes interested in programmed learning. Thus there is better teaching-learning so as to benefit every one.

THEORY OF PSYCHOLOGY

A psychological principle is one in which teaching is made effective by taking into account the psychology of the child. These principles are framed by keeping in mind the abilities, aptitudes, capacities and potentialities of the learners. They are formulated from the students point of view only. They would always create interest in the child for learning.

The desire to learn not only makes his learning more effective and easier but it also helps him to retain the subject matter in mind for a longer time. These principles include every psychological method which will help to improve the learning of the child. For example, principle of feedback and reinforcement is based on the laws of learning where reinforcement has always been given a lot of importance for learning. Further psychology has told that in a group a child will always learn better, thus the principle of utilizing group dynamics has been framed. Similarly, Psychology has always laid emphasis on rest and recreation and on it also a principle has been formulated.

VARIOUS LANGUAGES

1. General principles are followed by the teachers to make teaching-learning process effective whereas the Psychological Principles take the help of motivation of the students.
2. General Principles cover a wide range as compared to the Psychological principles which work within limited range.

A few Psychological principles of teaching are explained here below:

Principle of Motivation: Teaching is a tripolar process which involves the interaction of the teacher, the taught and the subject matter. For this, cooperation between the teacher and the taught is a must. Now the concept of teaching-learning has changed. It is no longer a process of teaching only. The emphasis has now shifted from the teacher to the learner. The important thing is to see whether the learner cooperates, whether his interest is there. The teacher's job is to motivate the learner by creating different situations of his interest. Motivation, therefore, is of supreme importance. How to motivate the learners is the pertinent issue.

The children are interested in their surroundings. The teacher should, therefore, provide to them that type of material. Some problems linked with their life situations may be put forth. The learners will try to be inside that problem and make all efforts to find out its proper solution.

The students should, therefore, be motivated towards the topic. The teacher has to teach. It is motivation which will make them interested in the topic and they actively participate in the class. Better learning on the part of students will be there if they are motivated towards that topic.

Environment of the class can be changed to break the monotony of the class. Aids can be used for the smaller children and for the matured students. Previous knowledge testing can be a potent motivation. For example, while teaching English grammar, the teacher should first explain the importance and need of learning English in present day world-how English can help them choose a better career and how it can be helpful for securing a good job. In this way, the students will be motivated to learn English well. Undoubtedly, motivation and interest are the two central factors in any process of teaching and learning.

Principle of Repetition and Exercise: The teacher should repeat several times what he teaches in the class so that the learners are able to grasp and understand the subject matter well. It also helps them to retain it in their minds for a longer time. Exercises for further practice may also be given as class work or as home assignment. It was Thorndike who put experimental evidences in favour of utility of repetition and exercise in the learning process.

Practice makes a man perfect. The students will fully grasp a thing when they are in a position to do it themselves. It needs a lot of practice on the part of the students. The teacher who makes use of exercises like revision, recapitulation, application of what has been taught to the students etc. can teach the students efficiently.

While teaching Geometry, the teacher asks the students to draw various triangles (isosceles, equilateral and right angled). He then asks them to measure the angles of those triangles and find out the sum of all the three angles of a triangle. It will obviously be equal to 180' in all the three cases. He will then repeat by giving some more examples of other triangles with different angles. Then the teacher may give more questions of similar type as home work.

Principle of Feedback and Reinforcement: During teaching the teacher should try to give positive reinforcement to the students. Some sort of feedback helps the students to learn things better. The knowledge of results should also be given to the learners side by side and as quickly as possible. Thus a weak student is able to know his drawbacks and then he can re-learn things and prepare himself again for further studies. By giving immediate results to the students, the teacher can also judge about his own teaching. Accordingly he can improve his teaching. During teaching, the teacher should try to encourage students as far as possible. It helps in developing a congenial environment.

Suppose the teacher during teaching has put a question to the class and no student is coming forward to give the response. The teacher should encourage the students and make them think and give the answer. The teacher in no case should discourage the child even if the answer is totally wrong. He should never say that the class is dull or the students are hopeless cases. He should show leadership in class and try to imbibe the qualities of leadership in the students.

Principle of Variety: The principle of variety is the foundation for better teaching-learning process. The teacher should try to bring variety in the class-room teaching. He should not use the same method of teaching always. For teaching, different methods at different times may be used. Suppose the teacher wants to correct the note-books of the students he can use different methods of correction work at different times.

Principle of Rest and Recreation: Fatigue decreases the speed of learning. There is need of giving rest after some interval of time. Study followed by rest and recreation refreshes the mind and prepares the learners for more studies. So the teacher should see that during teaching there should be provision for rest and recreation. Off and on some recreation activities may be organised in the class. That way class-room boredom will be ended.

Principle of Readiness: If a person is not ready to learn anything then teaching whatever it may be, cannot take place effectively. Readiness on the part of the learner is essential. As soon as the teacher enters into the class he should try to judge the readiness of the students. In case they are not ready then it is the duty of the teacher to make them ready. If the teacher takes care of this principle, then only his teaching comes out to be effective.

Principle of Fostering Creativity: During teaching the teacher should foster creativity among the students. He should always discourage cramming or reproduction of the material by them. In the class-room situations there are some students who cram the material, reproduce it and try to win the applause of the teachers.

The teacher should be able to judge about this type of students. There are some other students who are of creative type. He should encourage them to the maximum. In fact, the best teaching is one which always fosters the creativity among the carriers.

Principle of Sympathy and Cooperation: During teaching the teacher should possess sympathetic attitude and a cooperative bent of mind. Usually the students are afraid of the teacher. A good teacher is affectionate and tries to understand every student. He shows fatherly affections and motherly cooperation to his students. Whatever may be the situation, a good teacher remains sympathetic and affectionate.

Principle of Self-learning: A good teacher encourages the self-efforts made by the students for learning anything. He teaches in such a way so that the learners acquire the habit of self-learning. The teacher no longer believes in spoon feeding while teaching. He may start with lecture method but gradually he takes the students to self-learning situations. He remains there in the background helping and guiding them wherever they need some help or guidance.

Principle of Group-dynamics: The teacher should understand group-dynamics. He should try to inculcate among the learners a suitable type of group-behaviour. For this purpose he does his job of teaching in such a way so that he succeeds in making his students well behaved in every type of situation-may be as individual or in a group.

The children learn better in a group. They are also able to develop qualities of tolerance, cooperation, sacrifice etc. The teacher should therefore, encourage group learning.

Two

ART OF ENGLISH TEACHING

THEORY OF MEANING

Now, we would like to discuss in detail the theory of meaning that can be attributed to Firth and Halliday. Firth's ideas on meaning (seem to) have been largely influenced by Malinowski's ideas and the ancient Indian theories of meaning. Firth says that the complete meaning of a word is always contextual, and no study of meaning independent of a complete context can be taken seriously. He adds that each word when used in a new context is a new word. He emphasizes that the disciplines and techniques of linguistics are directed to assist us in making statements of meaning. Firth says that meaning has to be regarded as a complex of contextual relations, and phonetics, grammar, lexicography and semantics each handles its own components of the complex in its appropriate context.

Meaning is a cover term to account for the following functions:

1. Phonetic function
2. Lexical function

3. Morphological function
4. Syntactic function
5. Context of situation (semantic function).

PHILOSOPHICAL VIEW

Firth's ideas presented above have been adopted and well developed by Halliday, Ellis, Dixon and several other linguists. We shall present here their ideas in a comprehensive framework with adequate modifications wherever found necessary.

For the sake of convenience, let us postulate the following different levels and interlevels at which we can analyse a language and account for its features and properties:

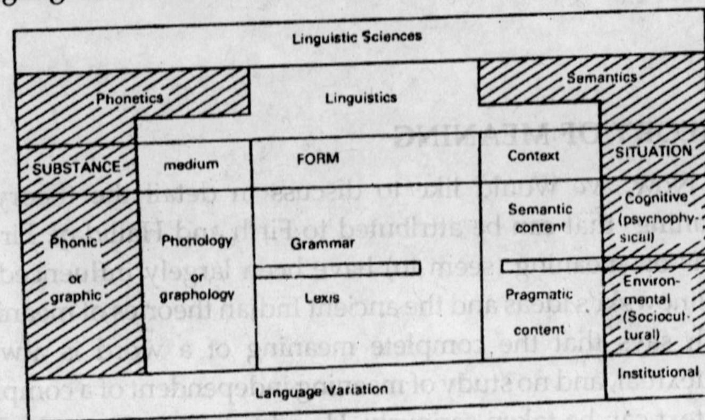

Fig. Levels of Linguistic Analysis

THE APPLICABILITY

Let us now look at the Functionalist approach of Hallidayan vintage. Here we shall look mainly at the 'content'—both semantic and pragmatic. The Hallidayan functional view of language takes the semantic structure as the central point-not the formal structure consisting of certain abstract syntatic structures.

A given utterance is viewed in terms of its 'meaning potential' and its lexicogrammatical actualization. The meaning (content) aspect is taken care of in terms of several functions and sub-functions:

I. Ideational
   (1) Experiential
   (2) Logical
II. Interpersonal
   (3) Rhetorical
   (4) Attitudinal
III. Textual
   (5) Thematic
   (6) Informational

We shall not get into the definitional aspects of these functions.

Let us look at these functions from the viewpoint of what we have termed as 'semantic content' and 'pragmatic content'. Let us workout a convenient way of keeping them apart. Semantic content is expounded by the lexicogrammar and phonology of language. Pragmatic content on the other hand is derived on the basis of the background-socio-cultural (wider situation) or (immediate) situational.

The experiential function of language with its participants, processes and circumstantials comes within the rubric of semantic content. Die logical function also comes under semantic content as far as the directly expounded features are concerned. But once we take the help of our knowledge of the external world to talk of an implicit relation we are drawing on what we, can call the 'pragmatic pool' (after 'presupposition pool' of Vennemann). Then that part of the content is pragmatic content. There are two interesting aspects to be discussed here. One, what is semantic in one context may be pragmatic in another context; and the other is that we can talk of the semantico-pragmatic threshold.

Let us talk of the semantic primes and pragmatic primes. The former are 'sememes' and the latter are 'pragmemes'. Whatever is 'denoted' by a lexical item directly will be a bundle of sememes and whatever is 'connoted' will be a cluster of pragmemes. Here inferences and suggestions will be included. Let us take two pairs of lexical items: (i) Master and Slave. (ii)Senior and Junior.

The lexeme 'slave' will have as one of its constituents the sememe [subservience]. On the other hand the lexeme junior' will not have it as its sememe. However, in certain contexts we might find a junior being expected to be subservient. In this case our information is from pragmeme [subservience]. In other words a given feature of content can be 'sememic' in one place and 'pragmemic' in another.

Let us look at the set of lexemes Master, husband, father, friend from the point of view of the feature [authority]. This feature will certainly be a sememe in the case of 'master' and a pragmeme in the case of 'friend'.

Between these two clear points we have 'father' and 'husband' where [authority] seems to be the semantico-pragmatic threshold: it is partly sememic and partly pragmemic. Their sememic-pragmemic ratio may differ between the two words and across cultures. In some cultures [authority] might simply be a pragmeme in all the three words.

One should of course keep in mind the problem of individual and societal variation regarding sememic and pragmemic values. It is very important to note that semantic change may consist mainly of interchange of sememes and pragmemes.

A pragmeme may operate at the rank of a lexeme or at the rank of a proposition. The study of pragmemes at the rank of lexeme may be considered lexical pragmatics and the study of pragmemes at the rank of proposition is propositional pragmatics. The pragmeme of [authority] has lexical origins.

On the other hand the feature [adult] is a propositional pragmeme used while comprehending the following sentence:

> John voted for the liberals.
>
> Let us now return to the functionalist viewpoint. The rhetorical sub-function, which takes care of 'mood' distinctions like interrogative and declarative, is semantic in nature because the relevant distinctions are 'worded' as it were-here 'wording' is used to include 'non-segmental phonologization' (prosodization) too. The attitudinal function which gets realized in the choice of lexical items and intonational features is also part of the semantic content. The textual function however seems to go in for both the 'pragmatic' and the 'semantic' rubrics. Wherever extrasentential or extralinguistic (phychological, cultural) reasons are to be brought in to explain certain choices we are within the pragmatic orchard. But on the other hand there are cases where certain lexicogrammatical and phonological features explain the thematic and informational choices-here we are within the semantic mansion. Here too one might be again on the threshold in certain cases. One thing is clear though some of the informational choices are overtly realized, but the triggering mechanism is not available in the immediate experience and is embedded in the socio-cultural melieu. Here pragmatics certainly stakes its claim.

We shall now try to look at three important concepts from the semantic and pragmatic grids:

> Presupposition
>
> Entailment
>
> Implication

Let us examine the following sentence:

1. Mohan is a bachelor.

This sentence may be said to have the following meanings attendant on it:

(a) Mohan is of marriageable age.

(b) Mohan is an adult.

(c) Mohan is yet to get married.

(d) Mohan will get married.

(e) Mohan may get married.

(f) Mohan may be trying to get married.

(a) is a pre-supposition triggered by the lexicogrammatical structure of the sentence itself, because the word 'bachelor' refers to someone who is not married but could have been married. But the word does not tell us anything of the age at which someone in a given society gets married. That only an 'adult' gets married is part of sociocultural information. So (b) draws its information from the pragmatic pool: hence it is pragmatic pre-supposition; (c) more or less is like the 'assertion' part of the content. It is semantic entailment. The fact that he will get married; (d) will be pragmatic entailment. That Mohan may get married is a legitimate aspect of futurology-hence it is semantic implication. The 'trying' part is not warranted by any part of the sentence; hence it is considered pragmatic implication. From (a) to (e) there seems to be a kind of sliding from the semantic pole to the pragmatic pole. The least semantic and the most pragmatic item is (e).

Bates rightly made the distinction between semantic and pragmatic pre-suppositions. There is a tendency among some to consider all pre-suppositions as pragmatic. What the code reflects is 'semantic' and what the encoder and decoder reflect is 'pragmatic'.

THE RECITAL

In our account of language, meaning is perceived at the level of 'Form' and the interlevels of 'medium' and 'context'. The medium of a given text can be either graphological or phonological. Meaning at this interlevel we shall call significance, which means 'phonological or graphological meaning'. Under the level of Form, we have two demilevels-grammar and lexas. The break in the dividing lines of grammar and lexas, and semantics and pragmatics is indicative of the clinal relationship between the members of each set. In other words one cannot make an absolute distinction between lexis and grammar and between semantics and pragmatics. The meaning we find within grammar and lexas we shall call Value. And finally meaning at the interlevel of context we shall call Content. Here, then, we have the following types of meaning:

1. phonological significance
   or
   graphological significance
2. (a) Grammatical value
   (b) Lexical value
3. (a) Semantic content
   (b) Pragmatic content.

Interlevel: The interlevel of context establishes relationship between the situational features and the formal items or categories (lexicogrammatical items). The situational features may be said to be of three types.

(i) the cognitive (psychophysical)
(ii) the environmental (sociological)
(iii) the institutional.

The cognitive level (sub- or demi-level) gives us information about the speaker's (and the hearer's) conceptualization of the real world phenomena (participants, processes, circumstantials, logical relations, informational and discoursal features).

Environmental Level: The environmental level is related to the cultural representation of the world phenomena. It includes a given speaker's attitude, temperament, mood and the like and the presence of the physical objects at the time of speech act. The cognitive level material gets reflected to a large extent in the semantic layer of the contextual interlevel. The environmental level material gets reflected in the pragmatic layer of the contextual interlevel. Semantic and pragmatic layers are like Siamese twins. One is tempted to agree with George Lakoff that pragmatics and semantics are inseparable (1973).

Institutional Level: The institutional level is a paralinguistic or extra-linguistic level which accounts for language variation at the interlevels and the level of Form. It takes care of distinctions like dialect, sociolect, register, and style. Any formally (lexicogrammatically) valuable construction will yield 'acceptable content' when it is studied with reference to all these features, though certain sentences might demand a lot of imagination to find them a pragmatic and thence semantic placement/ contentification.

Delicate Statements: When we talk of these levels we can also make more delicate statements (of superordinate-subordinate nature). The situation (i) could be immediate (x) or wider (y). The immediate cognitive situation will give us 'thesis'. By thesis is meant the event, process, action, state of affairs, etc., to which a given utterance refers. Ellis rightly calls it as the component creating 'a secondary universe' (I x) to the 'primary 'universe' (I y). The thesis of the utterance "(he is) running" can be said to be one of the existence and realization of the concept of 'swift movement'—this analysis is at a particular point on the scale of delicacy which means one can get at more delicate descriptions of this movement. The wider situation, that is, the 'universe' of the given utterance involves broader concepts like 'movement' and 'non-movement'.

The environmental (sociological) level too yields several subclasses on the immediate (x) and wider (y) dimensions. The other dimensions that are important are given the following labels: (a) topic, (b) personalities. With these dimensions, we will get the following features.

2 xa - motive	2 ya - motif
2 xb - roles	2 yb participants.

The 'motif' of an utterance like "how do you do" is one of maintaining certain courtesies and the 'motive' is one of 'greeting at the time of first meeting'. In an expression like "How are we feeling today Mrs. James", the motif is enquiry and the motive is 'the enquiry which is personal, that too about the addressee herself' as contrasted with "How is your husband today, Mrs. James" (Ellis, 1966).

Incidentally, the thesis of both the statements is one of 'health' and the 'universe' involves concepts of health, ill health, well-being and the like. In the first sentence the personalities in wider situation (i.e., participants) are doctor or nurse and patient and in immediate situation (i.e. roles) are speaker (or 'wisher') and hearer ('wished). An intermediate point can be postulated on this scale of 'immediate' and 'wide' points where, in this case, we can have the 'performer' and the 'non-performer'.

The features of the 'institutional' built on the dimensions of dialect (a), sociolect (b), register (c), style (d) are as follows:

3 xa: dialect-choice;	3 ya: dialect-range.
3xb: sociolect-choice,	3 yb: sociolect-range.
3xc: register-choice;	3 yc: register-range.
3xd: style-choice,	3 yd: style-range.

PAYING ATTENTION

Dialect is a language variety on the dimension of 'local' origin of the performer. Sociolect is a language variety on the dimension 'status-cum-social' origin of the performer. Register is the language variety identified on the dimensions of (i) field-subject matter (province of reference), and (ii) role-conversation, literacy, etc. Style is a language variety identified on the dimensions of (i) 'formality' (e.g. formal, casual intimate, frozen, consultative), and (ii) mode (e.g. written, taperecorded, broadcast, etc.).

Meaning: By dialect-range is meant the total repertory of dialects of the performer, his idiolect classified from a dialect point of view. By dialect-choice is meant the particular dialect out of the performer's range to which the utterance may be assigned. The distinction of 'range' and 'choice' operates on the same lines with other language varieties too.

Let us now get into different types of meaning in greater detail. As we have stated above, the phonological or graphological meaning will be labelled significance. We can recognize three types of features in phonology/ graphology: 'ematic' 'sodic' and 'ational'. The alternate levels (not demilevels) yield us three features each:.

Demi-levels	*Immediate (x)*	*Wider (y)*	
Cognitive	thesis	universe	
Environmental	motive	motif	topic (a)
	role	participant	personalities (b)
Institutional	dialect choice	dialect range	(b) dialect (a)
	sociolect choice	sociolect range	sociolect (b)
	register-choice	register range	register (c)
	style-choice	style-range	style (d)

Fig.: The level of situation

All the above are situational categories which help us arrive at the 'content' of well-formed chunks of utterance with certain 'values' of their own.

	Phonology	*Graphology*
ematic	phonematic units	Graphematic units
sodic	prosodic features	Grosodic features
ational	Intonational features	Graphational features

Fig.: The interlevel of medium

Phonematic units are those which are abstracted by analysing the speech sounds of a given language. Graphematic units are those which are used in writing. 'ematic' units are those which have unisegmental value.

Graphematic units	Phonematic units
i	/i/
e	/e/
a	/ Y /
	/a/
	/o/

Here we have avoided the more abstract practice of separating syntagmatic features from their paradigmatic associates.

Prosodic features are those supersegmental (non-unisegmental) features which go with the syllables and feet of the phonological hierarchy.

'Stress' in English and 'tone' in Punjabi are prosodic features. We have separated the intonational features from prosodic features for several reasons. Neither phonematic units nor prosodic features expound content distinctions. But the intonational features help us distinguish between different types of utterance especially with reference to attitudes and 'mood' (question, statement), the phonematic and prosodic elements remaining the same.

Some prosodic features get represented in certain scripts and such features can be called 'grosodic features'. Nasalization in Sanskrit is a prosodic feature which gets represented in Devanagari script used for Sanskrit, e.g. The punctuation marks like /./, /,/ & /;/ are 'graphational' features because they are intended to reflect in writing intonational features. However it needs to be noted that all the graphational features current in a writing system may not reflect intonational features. If a writing system is revised so as to bring in good equation between the two sets of features it would be quite profitable.

The 'significance' of a language involves a systematic study of the phonematic units, the prosodic and the intonational features. The meaning of a phonematic unit is the consideration of its syntagmatic and paradigmatic possibilities. For example, in English the significance of [n] involves a study which leads to statements of the following type:

(i) it cannot occur initially

(ii) it occurs finally or before /k/ and /g/

(iii) it contrasts with non-nasal velars; / k/ and / g/

(iv) it contrasts with nasal non-velars /m/ and /n/.

To quote Ellis "the phonological (graphological) meaning of an item such as a term in a phonological system is its relation to other phonological items, its place in the total phonological system concerned" (1966: 80). Often we come across statements like "the contrast of presence of aspiration and its absence is meaningless in English". Such a distinction will be proved invalid when a phonetic description is given to an 'instance' of the phonematic unit in an utterance, and a prosodic feature will be imposed on the phonematic unit in such instantial description.

The absence or presence of aspiration will be indicative of the phonic environment or the non-native background of the speaker. In either case aspiration is 'significant'. Here 'significant' means much more than 'meaning changing' ability.

Let us now move over to 'value', the meaning of

grammatical categories. To quote Ellis again: "The formal meaning of a formal item or category, either grammatical or lexical, is its relation to other formal items or categories. Phonological and formal meaning correspond to the information of 'information theory' in being dependent on, and questionable in terms of, the number of oppositions in a given system". Dixon says that formal meaning is "the meaning of a piece of language with respect to its internal patternings". He further says: "Two items will be said to have different formal meanings if and only if they receive distinct descriptions in terms of the categories of grammar and lexis for the language to which they belong." To discuss the value of 'a grammatical unit' or 'a lexical item' we shall have to consider each on two axes-the syntagmatic and the paradigmatic.

On the syntagmatic axis, a grammatical unit (e.g. sentence, clause, group, word, morpheme) has certain colligational privileges i.e. it has certain 'patterns' and structural possibilities. For example in English clause 'goal' or 'actor' can be 'subject' whereas 'attribute' or 'range' cannot be. An item in a 'system' will have one kind of value when it colligates with a particular item from another system and the value changes when it colligates with a different item. The value of a clause will be one when it has a goal complement and it will be different when it has a range complement. In the first case the clause of that structure will have a 'receptive' counterpart (or 'allosentence' or 'agnate clause', whereas the second one cannot:

(i) (a) He walked a horse (operative).
    (b) A horse was walked by him (receptive).

(ii) (a) He walked ten miles.
    (b) Ten miles was walked by him.

The value of 'walk' is different in these clauses. It is determined by its place in the system of verbal group. This consideration is on paradigmatic axis. A 'system' is a closed set of features which are distinct from one another. An item from the system enters into a particular structure. This is a colligational restriction. For example, a passive verbal group cannot be followed by a 'complement/ actor' but can be by an 'adjunct/ actor'.

sub/goal	passive pre-dication/ process	adjunct/ actor
(iii) The song	was sung	by John
sub	predicator	comp
(iv) the song	was sung	John

The second utterance will be acceptable if 'John' is "complement/ beneficiary"

Lexical Item: A lexical item is "a formal item (at least one morpheme) whose pattern of occurrence can be described in terms of uniquely ordered series of other lexical items occurring in its environments". A lexical item will have a 'scatter'. For example, the item 'strong' has the following scatter: strong, strongly, strength, strengthen, stronger, strongest. It has on the chain the possibility of co-occurring with items like 'argument' and 'tea', and has partial choice relationship with 'powerful'.

strong argument

strong tea

powerful argument

powerful tea

Important Observations: We shall now note here three important observations of Halliday regarding lexis:

1. Lexis seems to require the recognition merely of linear co-occurrence together with some measure of significant proximity, either a scale or at least a cut off point. It is this syntagmatic relation which is referred to as 'collocation'.... In the place of grammatical closed system, lexis requires open-ended 'set' assignment to

which is best regarded probabilistic. Collocation and lexical set are mutually defining as are structure and system. The set is the grouping of members with like privilege of occurrence in collocation.

2. In grammar, a 'bridge' category is required between the element of structure and the term in the system on the one hand and the formal item on the other and this is the class. But in lexis the item is directly referable to the categories of collocation and set.
3. The lexical item is not necessarily coextensive on either axis with the item, or rather with any of the items, identified and accounted for in the 'grammar'. So it may he useful to recognize, on the syntagmatic axis, a lexical item which has defined status in the grammar and is not identified as morpheme, word, or group, e.g. 'let in for', 'come out with'. Viewed from this angle a lexical item can be simple, compound or phrasal.

The meaning of a lexical item (value) will be a statement on the following parameters:

1. type of the lexical item: simple, compound, phrasal
2. scatter
3. collocational span or range
4. lexical set.

All formal patterns have certain 'value' as they enter into 'patterns' and 'systems' grammatically and 'ranges' and 'sets' lexically. A statement of 'value' of a formal item will therefore consist in the discussion of its 'grammatical' and 'lexical' properties, possibilities of co-occurrence and its restrictions, and of substitutability and its restrictions. Once we know the 'significance' and 'value' of a piece of language, we will be ready to discuss its 'content' at the interlevel of context by relating it to the relevant features of situation. However it needs to be noted that we can get at the 'significance' and 'value' of the forms of a language only after observing their behaviour in actual speech situations. So the process is recursive and bidirectional.

The contextual meaning of a piece of language is its meaning with respect to the correspondence that can be set up between its internal patterns and the relevant patterns in its general situation. Ellis rightly says that we can formulate 'content' as a network of relations within context, systemic and structural ones of the 6 value' type.

All formal items, both grammatical items and lexical items, have contextual meaning. The situational features which we have noted above are 'universal' categories. What differs for different languages is the selection of situational features made by the different systems of contextual meaning. Our situation is the same as Hjelmslev's 'content substance' and our context is similar to his 'content form'. Content is either potential or instantial (actual).

The potential content of a formal item is the range of possible contents of that item considered in abstraction from any text. Its instantial content is the actual content in a given instance of occurrence in a given place in a given text with a given situation. Ellis postulates between two extremes a line of 'potentiality/ instantiality', and associated with it is the scale of delicacy of focus. He says that the utterance (instantial meaning) is the unit of form related to situation.

On the basis of utterance and the formal categories of a given language we can abstract the categories of the context of the given language (potential meaning). The unit of form related to context is the potential utterance, and here the minimal unit is the sentence. Here one can refer to Antal's viewpoint: "The sentence is the minimum unit of content and at the same time the maximum unit of the meaning." Antal's 'meaning' is similar to our 'value'. He says that 'meaning' unites the form of the sentence (its signs) and the content of the sentence and that it explains the observable regularity in the use of signs.

The scale of potentiality and instantiality is also associated with the scale of 'notion'. The more delicate the notion is, the nearer we are to the 'instantial' meaning. The delicacy of focus is the relation between contextual meaning and thesis or between contextual meanings.

The situational relation tn< ts (= a lesser time than before) yields the contextual meaning tR=past (R=reference, potential contextual meaning corresponding to thesis)

tn ts: tR = future

tn = ts: tR = present (i.e., non (exclusively) past/ future)

where = is a relation other than exclusively before or after, including (includes) and > (before and after). Ellis describes the 'tense' aspect of the utterance.

They'll have been going to have been building a National theatre for ten years now as follows:

$tn_1 > ts,\ tn_2 < tn_1,\ tn_3 > tn_2,\ tn_4 < tn_3,\ tn_5\ \ tn_4.$

Dixon generalizes that the elements from successive matrices associated with successive processes of language in a text will correspond to contextual descriptions which are consistent with one another and in which a chain of continuity can be recognized. Ambiguity cannot be present if the 'value' of a formal item and its 'situation' were allowed to be scientifically relevant to its linguistic consideration. A given chunk of utterance will be assigned its content if we are given the 'wider' and 'immediate' features of the situation in which the piece was uttered.

To sum up the contextual approach to meaning we note the following points:

(i) 'Meaning' has to be discovered at different levels and interlevels of linguistic analysis.

(ii) At each level or interlevel we have to analyse an utterance in terms of units and features and account for its properties of co-occurrence and its restrictions, and substitutability and its restrictions.

(iii) 'Meaning' which falls within the range of linguistics will be at the level of Form and the interlevels of Medium and Context.

THE CONVERSATION

According to Firth we establish ourselves on speaking terms with our environment, and our words serve our familiarity with it. "The study of words in cultural familiarity" describes the semantic aspect of language. This theme is recurrent in Firthian writings. "To begin with, we must apprehend language events in their contexts as shaped by the creative acts of speaking persons". There is an association of social and personal attitude in recurrent contexts of situation with certain phonological features.

Collocation is an important concept of the Firthian theory of semantics. Meaning by collocation is an abstraction at the syntagmatic level and is not directly concerned with the conceptual or idea approach to meanings of words. The collocations; can be normal or unique and personal or a normal. Firth uses the expression 'lower modes of meaning' to refer chiefly to the handling of meaning at the phonetic, phonological, prosodic and grammatical levels of abstraction. He proposes the following as the categories of the context of situation:

The relevant features of participants—persons and personalities:

(i) The verbal action of the participants.

(ii) The non-verbal action of the participants.

Three

TEACHING METHODS

In the process of learning and teaching, a method of teaching is very important. The teacher with a good method of teaching is liked by the students. A good method of teaching results into good learning. A good teacher is always in search of an effective method of teaching. A method tells the teacher how the matter should be taught. It is a tool in the hands of a teacher.

A method is a servant and not master. A good teacher tries to take out best out of it. Selection of the right method ensures success of the teacher. It helps in the achievement of goals.

Let us first of all know what is a method? In a method, the word 'how' is important. Thus in a method we come to know how should something be presented.

According to *W.F. Mackey*, "A method determines what and how much is taught (Selection), the order in which it is taught (Gradation), how the meaning and form are conveyed (Presentation) and what is done to make the use of the language unconscious. Thus we find that a method deals with form of things that is selection, gradation, presentation and repetition."

If we go back to the old days, we find that nobody was so particular about the method of teaching. But this does not mean that at that time no method was being used. They followed certain methods surely. But a method has become a problem in this age of scientific approach. The questions, what should be taught and how it should be taught, are intimately connected. "Methods are meant for us and not we for the methods. The methods are to serve us in our teaching process and hence to be our servants and not our master".

DIFFERENT METHODS

Bilingual method means a method where two languages i.e., the mother tongue and target language are used. Here the mother tongue is used to achieve the target language. This method is based on the similarities and differences which exist between the two languages. The similarities and differences may be of situation, sounds, vocabulary, structure etc. If these differences or common things are known well, then learning of a foreign language is facilitated considerably when the child is learning his mother tongue, he becomes familiar with the situations and picks up the language correctly. While learning the foreign language, the situations are created again in order to make the child learn the foreign language. The advocates of bilingual method believe that it is merely wastage of time as there is duplicity of, the same thing. Of course, mother tongue equivalents he told but there is no need of re-creating the situations. It is suggested that the time thus saved may be utilised for giving practice in sentence patterns.

DIRECT APPROACH

Direct Method of teaching English means teaching English directly through English medium. In this method, mother tongue is not used at all. This method came as a reaction against the translation method. It is also called the natural method of teaching. No doubt, large number of teachers are in favour of translation method but even then, there are many others who like to follow the direct method. The main philosophy behind this method is that the learner learns a foreign language in the same way as he learns his mother tongue.

According to Webster's New International Dictionary, "Direct method is a method of teaching a foreign language, especially a modern language through conversation, discussion and reading, in the language itself, without the use of pupil's language, without translation and without the study of formal grammar. The words are first taught by pointing to object or picture or by performing actions." Some language experts are of the opinion that the direct method is not a method at all. *Prof. Gurrey* says, "But essentially it (The Direct Method) is a principle, not a teaching method, a system that operates through many methods; a way of handling the new language and of presenting to the class. It demands direct bond, that is, a direct association, between word and thing and between sentence and idea instead of an indirect one through the mother tongue."

Basic Principles of the Method

The basic principles on which this method is based are briefly given below:

(a) *Direct Association between Thought and Words:* In this method, the learners think and speak by using the same medium.

(b) *Oral Practice:* A lot of oral practice is a must for even, one, is the basis of this method.

(c) *Functional Grammar:* In this method, stress is laid on functional grammar and not on theoretical grammar.

(d) *Inhibition of Mother Tongue:* This method propagates the teaching of the foreign language without using mother tongue.

(e) *Sentence as the Unit of Speech:* Here the unit of speech is a sentence and not a -word. Emphasis is laid on speaking full sentences.

(f) *Limited Vocabulary:* This method favours the presentation of limited vocabulary, based on needs and experiments of the learners.

The Advantages: The following are the advantages of this method:

1. This method lays more emphasis on oral work. That ensures good pronunciation to the learners.
2. For teaching the idioms of English, this method is more suitable.
3. There is direct bond between thought and expression. So it helps the learner to have fluency in speech. It helps the students to have good command over the language.
4. Psychologically, this method is very sound because the teacher proceeds from particular to general and from concrete to abstract.
5. It makes the teaching of English easy and pleasant.
6. It helps the teacher and the learner to cover up more syllabus in less time.

The Disadvantages

(1) There is need of really competent teachers for teaching English by using this method. But we have dearth of such teachers. Sometimes the teacher fails to make the students understand the meaning of a particular word because the use of mother tongue is not allowed.

(2) In this method, there is over emphasis on oral work. Reading and writing process of the language get less attention.

(3) This method, cannot be used successfully for the average and the below average students.

(4) It is an expensive method because the teacher has to use some aids for teaching.

(5) This method does not lay emphasis on the selection and gradation of language material which is very important.

(6) At the early stages, sometimes this method may fail miserably.

The students may not be able to learn anything.

Thus we find that the direct method of teaching has some shortcomings, but its merits cannot be ignored. On the whole, it is considered to be a good method for teaching English. The best thing for the teachers would be to modify it according to the needs and requirements of the learners.

STRUCTURE AND PATTERN

Heavily debated in the term 'Structural Approach' as it stands, because some people misinterpret it. They believe that it is a method of teaching English. The hard fact is that it is not a method. In a method, we come to know how a particular item is to be taught. In fact, a method is a body of certain techniques. Besides, methods vary from person to person, from place to place and from subject to subject but in case of an approach, we do not have any such type of alternatives. In structural approach, the different structures form the most important thing. Any method can be used for presenting the structures to the learners. Thus we find that the structural approach is not a method but it is an approach which quickens the process of learning a language.

The expression 'Structural Approach' comprises two words 'structural' and 'approach'. The word 'Structural' relates to the structures and 'Approach' literally means coming near. Thus Structural Approach in teaching of English means approaching English on the basis of structures. For this purpose, the structures are well made to teach English. That is called

Structural Approach. In this approach, the structures are taught by creating situations. That makes the teaching, learning more effective.

Menon and Patel say in their book 'The Teaching of English as a Foreign Language.' "The Structural approach is based on the belief that in the learning of a foreign language, mastery of structures is more important than the acquisition of vocabulary."

Various Approaches

Different approaches for teaching English are vocabulary approach, grammar approach, structural approach, functional approach etc. In vocabulary approach, the students learn vocabulary items and thereby try to learn English. It is not very effective because words in isolation are not effective for learning the language. In grammar approach, the students are asked to learn the rules of grammar. That does not help much in learning the language. In structural approach, structures are taught by creating situations. All efforts are made to help the students have mastery over the structures. Comparatively structural approach is more effective in teaching a language. In functional approach, functions of the language are given importance. These days communicative function of the language is given the top most importance.

Structure Definition

The different arrangements in one accepted style or the other is called a structure. The structure may be a complete utterance or it may be a part of some large pattern. The different types of arrangements are called structures. The structures are the tools of a language. Every language has its own tools; its own pattern of structures. The structures are just like photo frames. Once we get a photo frame, any number of photos can be fitted into it. In the same way, if we learn a structure any number of sentences of the same type can be constructed.

Here below are examples of some structures:

I. S.V.O.

(a) We bought books. (b) She played hockey.
(c) I knew him. (d) The police caught the thief.
(e) You learnt a lesson. (f) He taught English.

II. V.S.O.

(a) Is he a doctor? (b) Are you Geeta?
(c) Is it a flower? (d) Was she a lecturer?
(e) Was it a dog? (f) Was-she a doctor?

III. S.V.O (Negative)

(a) He is not a doctor. (b) You are not Geeta.
(c) It is not a flower. (d) Veena is not a teacher.

IV. V.S.O. (Negative)

(a) Is he not a doctor? (b) Are you not Geeta?
(c) Is it not a flower? (d) Is your brother not a doctor?
(e) Is she not a teacher?

Different Kinds

There are different types of structures. Basically we may divide them into four different categories:

Sentence Patterns: The sentences may be of different designs e.g., He is my friend. Is he a thief? He has not accepted my proposal. Roshan was not my friend.

Formula: Formula means group of words used regularly on certain occasions e.g., Good evening. Thank You, That's right, Mention not, Good-bye.

Phrase Patterns: The different types of phrases are in the house, out of pocket, under the chair, on the table etc.

Idioms: These are the group of words that must be taught as a whole and not as separate ones, e.g., in the teeth of, in black and white, at sixes and sevens, a snake in the grass etc.

The Meaning

Approaching English on the basis of selected structures is called Structural Approach. It is called structural approach because the main emphasis is laid on the mastery of structures or pattern of sentences and phrases and also on the special features of the language which help in the construction of a sentence such as word order, structural words and a few inflexions in English.

In this approach, the use of mother tongue is allowed at the initial stages and that too for explaining a situation when some sentence pattern is to be practised.

But it does not allow translation of the structures which are to be practised. The learners are given drill of the structures till they are able to use them automatically without straining their minds.

By teaching the different structures, the aim is to develop certain skills. The different skills are as under:

Ability to (i) understand the spoken language

(ii) speak the language

(iii) read the language

(iv) write the language

In structural approach, the emphasis is on the acquisition of different skills. The person learning the language is able to acquire it through situations. *E.V Gatenby* says: "First follow nature is a good piece of advice for the language teacher. As nature does show us a sure way to success it is only common sense to follow her methods. Where they are followed today in the schools of the world, there is very little failure to learn a language."

The Goals

According to *Menon* and *Patel*, the objectives of structural approach are:

1. To lay the foundation of English by establishing thorough drill and repetition about 275 graded structures.

2. To enable the children to attain mastery over an essential vocabulary of about 3000 root words for active use.
3. To correlate the teaching of grammar and composition with the reading lessons.
4. To teach the four fundamental skills namely understanding, speaking, reading and writing in the order named.
5. To lay proper emphasis on the aural oral approach, active methods and the condemnation of formal grammar for its own sake.

THE VARIATIONS

In comparison with translation method, the bilingual method stands unique because in this case, we have some modification of translation method. In this method, mother tongue is used by the teacher only, and that too for explaining the meaning of difficult words and not by the students. Secondly, the students get a lot of practice in patterns which is not taken care of in translation method.

The Advantages

1. The teacher is able to teach English to the entire satisfaction of the learners.
2. The students are able to understand English well.
3. Judicious use of mother tongue by the teacher does not spoil the environment of teaching English. It only helps in teaching English.
4. It helps in giving proper training for different skills i.e., listening, speaking, reading and writing. Pattern practice given to the learners is essential in acquiring a skill.
5. The use of mother tongue saves a lot of time otherwise the teacher will have to make use of number of devices for giving meanings of words. Meanings and concepts

conveyed in this way are better understood by the learners.

6. It helps in developing fluency in spoken language.

The Comparison: In Indian situations, many a time the Direct Method of teaching English creates problems. Sometimes the teacher finds it difficult to make the student understand and sometimes the student fails to follow properly. Bilingual method is, that way, a very good remedy. In Direct Method, no body is allowed to use mother tongue in any situation whereas in the Bi-lingual method some freedom is there for the teacher. He/She may use mother tongue where the situation demands it. In some situation where the student has failed to follow the teacher inspite of the best efforts made by the teacher, mother tongue may be used. Thus the glaring drawbacks of the Direct Method have been put to end by the use of the Bi-lingual method. Moreover, the merits of the Direct method continue in the Bi-lingual method.

7. This method does not need special facilities or equipment. It can be successfully used anywhere and everywhere.
8. Teachers of English also love to teach by this method as it does not burden their mind with extra tabour.
9. It fully makes use of the language habits already acquired by the learners while learning their mother tongue.

The Disadvantages

(1) In Bilingual method, the teacher teaches English through English medium and in certain situations he starts using mother tongue. It diverges the attention of the learners.

(2) A teacher of English may not be good in both the languages. Whatever mother tongue he uses in the class while teaching English, may not be upto the mark.

It may leave bad impression of the teacher on the learners.

(3) The use of mother-tongue while teaching English spoils the continuity and fluency of language.

(4) A few students in the class may be more attentive to mother tongue sound and less attentive to English sounds. Their pronunciation may become defective.

(5) While contrasting the features of the two languages, there is possibility of confusion.

(6) The bad habit of learning everything by filtering through mother tongue may be formed.

(7) This method may degenerate into pure translation method if the teacher fails to handle it properly.

Which Method is the Best? Having discussed the various methods of teaching English in India, we come to the conclusion that there is something good, something bad in each method. None of the methods is perfect in every respect. This does not mean that we shall give up the use of all these methods. We must use one method or the other but the point to be taken care of is that a teacher should use the method as long as it (method) is a slave to him and he is able to do well with it. But when the teacher becomes a slave to the method, the whole teaching work becomes a hotch-potch. So it is rather advisable that the teacher should adopt eclectic and pragmatic approach because no single approach is useful in all the situations.

The technique of teaching is important but at the same time we must say that the material is not of less importance. The success of teaching-learning depends upon the technique as well as the choice of material. The material required and the method to be used for it always depend upon a number of factors which are mentioned below:

1. The learner-his age, level of learning, capacity, interest etc.

2. The teacher-his efficiency, insight, training etc.
3. The objectives of teaching English.
4. Class in which its study is introduced.
5. Availability of different types of aids.
6. Size of the class.
7. Location of the institution.
8. Social background etc.

GRAMMAR VS TRANSLATION METHOD

The Translation Method is better known as the Grammar-Translation Method. It is also called the classical method of teaching English. In the teaching of English as foreign language, it has enjoyed a great reputation in the past. At present also, many teachers prefer to teach English by this method. It the past Greek, Latin, French, German etc. were taught by this method. Translation method means teaching the target language by translating it into mother tongue-may be Hindi or Punjabi. Here each phrase or sentence of English is taught by translating it into mother tongue. The philosophy behind this method is that the foreign language can be best taught or learn through translation. The learners, however, have to make use of set rules and principles of grammar.

The Principles: The Grammar Translation method is based on the following principles:

(a) Teaching of a foreign language through translation is easy, quick and economical.

(b) The structural patterns of the two languages are compared and this comparison makes learning more clear and firm.

(c) The fundamental principle of proceeding from known to unknown is followed throughout.

(d) The knowledge of rules helps the learners to avoid any type of mistakes.

The Advantages: The grammar translation method has a number of advantages which are given below:

(1) This method is very successful in the present day class-rooms, where there are a large number of students in each section.

(2) By telling the meaning of a word or sentence in mother tongue, the teacher can at once make the students understand. Thus it is less time consuming.

(3) It is very reliable for giving the students practice of reading with understanding.

(4) In this method, the teacher as well as the learners are able to facilitate the teaching-learning process.

(5) Teaching English by using this method does not require lot of labour on the part of the teacher. Thus many teachers who are not habitual of working hard feel happy.

(6) By using this method, the comprehension of the students can be tested very easily.

(7) The learners are able to learn many items of English by comparison with mother tongue. That makes learning more clear and firm.

The Disadvantages

1. This method ignores the practice of oral work to the students which is the most important aspect in the teaching of any language.
2. In this method, reading comes first and speaking afterwards. That is very unnatural,
3. This method wastes a lot of time of student because everything has to be translated compulsorily.
4. The translation work is always approximate. So the learner is not able to learn things accurately.
5. Through translation work, the real spirit of meanings contained in the sentence is missed.

6. It does not provide opportunity for silent reading.
7. It lays more emphasis on rules of grammar which is not very sound in teaching-learning of a language.
8. This method makes the students think in mother tongue and then translate the same into English. In many cases, it may lead to funny expressions for example:- The road began to walk.
9. It is a dull and mechanical method because the learner remains passive mostly.
10. It does not help the students to learn correct pronunciation of English.
11. The learners can remain absent minded while being taught by this method. Many a time they just try to show their teacher that they are listening to him.
12. This method does not help the students to learn the language.

Thus we find that the grammar translation method has a few merits and more draw-backs. But even then we find that it has gained universal popularity. It is being used by a large number of teachers. One of the reasons of deteriorating standards of English is the use of this type of method. The best thing would be not to use translation method as such in the class rooms. It may be used only when the class-room situation demands it.

Four

AIMS OF TEACHING ENGLISH

For carrying out any activity it is significant to know its purpose. If the purpose is clear, the activity will be carried out effectively. If one knows clearly what is to be achieved the planning will be done accordingly and the work will be carried out properly. Even if it is not carried out properly at least it can be measured or evaluated as to what extent the activity has been successful. This (evaluation) is only possible by comparing the achievement of the activity with its planned purpose, goal or objectives.

In the same way in education or in any particular field of education the identification of goals, aims and objectives is a very important activity. Here the question is what should be the aims and objectives of science education and science teaching? Before knowing the aims and objectives of science education, as a teacher we should also know that aims and objectives of teaching of any subject should be directly related to the educational philosophy and policies. Educational philosophy and policies give justification for teaching various subjects in school including science.

Aims and objectives of science education have undergone many changes because the goals of education are also changing with the changes in the society.

The objectives of science education and science teaching have been stated by various educators, education commissions and committees, and in many different terms. We talk about goals, aims and objectives, etc., sometimes they are used as synonymous terms; and sometimes they are used in different meanings. Before discussing the aims and objectives of science teaching it will be helpful at this stage to distinguish between these terms.

BEHAVIOURAL OBJECTIVES

If you are keen in making lesson plans which may help you in achieving your identified objectives, they (the objectives) should be clearly stated. If objectives are not well defined, it is impossible to evaluate a student, a lesson, a unit, a course or a programme efficiently, and there is no sound basis for selecting appropriate material, content or instructional method.

Unless the teacher (or programmer) himself has a clear picture of his instructional intent, he will be unable to select test items or frame questions that clearly reflect the student's ability to perform the desired skills or demonstrate his acquisition of desired information. With clearly defined objectives, the student knows which activities on his part are relevant to his success.

A meaningfully stated objective is one that succeeds in communicating to the reader the writer's instructional intent. It is meaningful to the extent it conveys to others a picture (of what a successful learner will be like) the writer has in mind. For example, if you provide another teacher with an objective, and he then teaches his students to perform in a manner that you agree in consistent with what you have in mind, then you have communicated your objective in a meaningful manner.

Core Aspect

The best statement of the meaningful objective is the one that excludes the greatest number of possible alternatives to your objective. There are many needed words which are open to a wide range of interpretation. To the extent that you use such words, you have yourself open to misinterpretation, consider the following examples of words in this light.

Words Open to Many Interpretation — In order to understand, to really understand, to appreciate, to fully appreciate, to grasp the significance of, to enjoy, to believe, to have faith in, etc.

Words Open to Fewer Interpretation — to recite, to write, to identify, to differentiate, to solve, to construct, to list, to compare, to contrast, etc.

What do you mean when you say that you want a learner to know some thing? Do you mean that you want him to be able to recite, to solve, or to construct? Just to tell him you want him to know tells him little — the word can mean many things.

Though it is all right to include such words as 'understand' and 'appreciate' in a statement of objective, the statement is not explicit enough to be useful until it indicates how you intend to sample the 'understanding' or 'appreciating. Until you describe what the learner will be doing when demonstrating that he 'understands' or 'appreciates' you have described very little if you want him to do at all. Thus, the statement that communicates best will be one that describes the terminal behaviour of the learner well enough to avoid misinterpretation.

Attentive Behaviour

The most important characteristic of a useful objective is that it identifies the kind of *performance* that will be accepted as evidence that the learner has achieved the objective. The way to write an objective, that meets this requirement is to write a statement describing one of your educational intents and then modify it until it answers the question, "What is the learner doing when he is demonstrating that he has achieved the objective?" If the answer of this question is "YES" the statement of the objective will include the "Observable Behaviour" which the learner will be showing when he is demonstrating that he has achieved the objective.

The objective written in this manner is called Behavioural Objective. As for example 'to be able to solve quadratic equation' or 'to be able to repair a radio' are behavioural objectives which include the observable behaviours 'solve' and 'repair' respectively.

Let us see another objective. 'To develop an appreciation for music.' Now ask the same question "what is the learner doing when he is demonstrating that he has achieved the objective?"

1. Does he sigh in ecstasy when he is listening to music?
2. Does he buy a stereo system and records?
3. Does he correctly answer 95 per cent multiple choice questions on the history of music?
4. Does he write an essay on five musical instruments?
5. Does he say 'Oh Boy! It's too much.'

For every question the answer is No. It is not a behavioural objective.

Laws

To state an objective that will successfully communicate your educational intent you will sometimes have to define terminal behaviour further by stating the conditions you will impose upon the learner which he is demonstrating his mastery of the objective. Here are some examples:

1. Given a list of
2. Given any reference of learner's choice
3. Without the aid of references

4. Given a standard set of tools
5. Without the aid of tools
6. Without the aid of calculator.

As for example in the behavioural objective 'Given a list of 35 chemical elements, the learner must be able to recall and write the valances of at least 30/ 'to recall and write' is the observable behaviour and 'Given a list of 35 chemical elements' is the condition. Similarly the behavioural objective 'Given a linear algebraic equation, the learner must be able to solve for the unknown without the aid of references, tables or calculating devices' has both — the observable behaviour as well as the condition.

For conditions you should ask yourself questions like these:

1. What the learner will be provided?
2. What will the learner be deprived?
3. What are the conditions under which you will expect the terminal behaviour to occur?

Very often, a good way to explain to the learner the conditions under which he will be expected to perform is simply to show him some sample test.

Example:

(Behavioural objective stating observable behaviour and condition). The student must be able to demonstrate his understanding of the rules of logic by correctly solving problems of the following type: Which of the following statements is illustrated by the diagram below:

(a) All animals are birds

(b) Some birds are animals

(c) All birds are animals

(d) No birds are animals.

Answer, (c)

Ideal Sign

'What is it you want the learner to be able to do' gives the Observable Behaviour, and 'how will you want him to be able to do' given Criterion of acceptable performance. In order to include Criterion of acceptable performance in the statement of objective, indicate 'what the acceptable performance will be' by addition of words that describe the criterion of success.

Examples: (Behavioural objectives having criterion)

1. The student must be able to correctly solve at least seven simple linear equations within a period of 30 minutes.

Behaviour : Solve

Condition : within 30 minutes

Criteria : atleast 7

2. Given Human Skeleton, the student must be able to correctly identify by labelling at least 40 of the following bones; there will be no penalty for guessing (list of bones inserted here)

Behaviour : Identify

Condition : Given a human Skeleton

Criterion : at least 40

Condition and Criterion for Observable Behaviour: In order to test whether the statement of objective consists of *observable behaviour, condition* and *criterion,* the following questions may be asked:

1. Does the statement describe what the learner will be doing when he is demonstrating that he has reached the objective? (Behaviour)
2. Does the statement describe the important conditions (given or restriction or both) under which the learner will be expected to demonstrate his competence? (Condition)
3. Does the statement indicate how the learner will be evaluated?

Does it describe at least the lower limit of acceptable performance? (Criterion). These are the 3 items for stating Behavioural Objectives.

Various Dimensions

How can you write the behavioural objective having all the three items behaviour, conditions and criterion?

1. Identify the terminal behaviour by name, you can specify the kind of behaviour that will be accepted as evidence that the learner has achieved the objective.
2. Try to define the observed behaviour by describing the important conditions under which the behaviour will be expected to occur.
3. Specify the criteria of acceptable performance by describing how well the learner must perform to be considered acceptable.

Although each of these items might help an objective to be more specific, it will not be necessary to include all the three in each objective except observable behaviour.

1. A statement of instructional objective is a collection of words or symbols describing one of your instructional intents.
2. An objective will communicate your intent to the degree you have described what the learner will be doing when demonstrating his achievement and how you will know when he is doing it.
3. To describe the terminal behaviour (what the learner will be doing):
   (a) Identify and name the overall *behaviour* act.
   (b) Define the important *conditions* under which the behaviour is to occur (given or restrictions or both).
   (c) Define the *criterion* of acceptable performance.

4. Write a separate statement for each objective; the more statements you have the better chance you have of making clear your intent.
5. If you give each learner a copy of your objectives, you may not have to do much else.

Particular Aims

When stating objectives in behavioural terms, some keywords (called behavioural terms) are used. In the cognitive domain there are six categories of objectives — knowledge, comprehension, application, analysis, synthesis and evaluation (Chapter 3). The teachers should practise in writing behavioural objectives in all these categories. For convenience behavioural terms for each category are given below:

Knowledge: define, describe, identify, label, list, match, name, outline, reproduce, select, state.

Comprehension: convert, explain, extend, generalise, give example, infer, paraphrase, predict, rewrite, summarise.

Application: change, compute, demonstrate, discover, manipulate, modify, operate, predict, prepare, relate, show, solve, use.

Analysis: break down diagrams, differentiate, discriminate, distinguish, identify, illustrate, infer, outline, point out, relate, select, separate, subdivide.

Synthesis: categorise, combine, compile, compose, create, devise, design, explain, generate, modify, organise, plan, rearrange, revise, rewrite, summarise, tell, write.

Evaluation: appraise, compare, conclude, contrast, describe, discriminate, explain, justify, interpret, relate, summarise, support.

The Evaluation

When objectives are clearly defined and stated in behavioural terms, it is easy to develop test items (for multiple choice test items) for evaluation. Teachers should practise in constructing test items for identified objectives stated in behavioural terms.

Some sample test items developed on some behavioural objectives are given below:

SAMPLES TEST ITEMS

Topic: Structure of an Atom

Behavioural Objectives:

1. The students will identify the definition of atom with 100 per cent accuracy.
2. Given a list of material objects such as proton, positron, electron and neutron the students will identify the names of the particles of an atom with 100 per cent accuracy.
3. The students will write, how weights of electron, neutron and proton are related (weight of neutron is approximately equal to the weight of proton and weight of electron is negligible compared to the weight of proton and neutron) by memory with 100 per cent accuracy.
4. The students will write the charges of electron, proton and neutron (negative, positive, neutral) by memory with 100 per cent accuracy)
5. Given a diagram of atomic model the students will label the parts (shells) and nucleus with 100 per cent accuracy.
6. Given the number of protons and electrons in an atom the students will write the charge of that atom with 100 per cent accuracy.
7. The students will write the position of protons, neutrons, and electrons in the atom by memory with 100 per cent accuracy.

8. Given the number of protons and neutrons, the students will write the atomic weight of the element.
9. Given the number of electrons or protons in an atom, the students will write the atomic number of the element.
10. Given the number of particular shell (1st, 2nd....last, next to last) the students will write the maximum number of electrons in that shell with 100 per cent accuracy.
11. Given the atomic number and atomic weight of an element the students will write the number of electrons in various shells and the number of protons and neutrons in the nucleus with 100 per cent accuracy.

Test Items

1. The smallest unit of elements is a/an
   (a) electron (b) atom
   (c) molecule (d) proton
2. The atom consists of all the following except
   (a) electron (b) proton
   (c) positron (d) proton
3. The weight of neutron is approximately equal to the weight of
   (a) electron (b) proton
   (c) twice the proton (d) none of them
4. The weight of an electron is
   (a) equal to the weight of neutron
   (b) equal to the weight of proton
   (c) negligibly small
   (d) more than the weight of proton or neutron.
5. The charge of a proton is
   (a) positive (b) negative
   (c) neutral (d) sometimes negative and sometimes positive

6. A negatively charged atomic particle is
   (a) proton (b) electron
   (c) neutron (d) nucleus
7. A neutral particle of an atom is
   (a) electron (b) proton
   (c) neutron (d) nucleus
8. 'A' represents
   (a) shell (b) nucleus
   (c) both a and b (d) none of them
9. 'B' represents
   (a) shell (b) nucleus
   (c) both a and b (d) none of them
10. If an atom has 17 protons in its nucleus and 17 electrons in the shells the charge of the atom is
    (a) positive (b) negative
    (c) neutral (d) none of them
11. The nucleus of an atom has
    (a) protons only (b) neutrons only
    (c) neutral (d) none of them
12. Which of the particles are found outside the nucleus in an atom?
    (a) neutron (b) electron
    (c) proton (d) none of them
13. An element has 11 protons, 11 electrons and 12 neutrons. The atomic weight of the element is
    (a) 11 (b) 12
    (c) 22 (d) 23
14. An element has 8 electrons, 8 protons and 8 neutrons. The atomic number of the element is
    (a) 8 (b) 16
    (c) 24 (d) 36

15. An atom has 8 electrons. The number of electronsin its 2nd shell will be

(a) 2 (b) 6

(c) 8 (d) 18

16. The atomic number of an element is 17 and its atomic weight is 35. All of the following statements are correct except

(a) the nucleus will have 17 protons and 18 neutrons

(b) the nucleus will have 18 protons and 17 neutrons

(c) the first shell will have 2 electron

(d) the third shell will have 7 electrons.

ANSWERS

1. (b)	2. (c)	3. (b)	4. (c)
5. (a)	6. (b)	7. (c)	8. (b)
9. (a)	10. (c)	11. (c)	12. (b)
13. (d)	14. (a)	15. (b)	16. (b)

LEARNING OBJECTIVES

Once a teacher decides to teach his students, he plans several activities for a successful lesson. First he decides the topic, secondly he prepares objectives to be achieved, then he decides a relevant methodology to achieve the identified objectives. Finally he plans to evaluate student's performance.

Objectives are identified and written in various different forms. Some teachers believe that their students should "really understand" others desire that their students should know some scientific laws, facts and principles.

Some desire that their students should "internalise knowledge," and still others want that their students should grasp the core or essence or comprehend. Do they all mean the same thing?

To clarify such confusions and help all teachers, administrators, professional, specialists and research workers who deal with curricular and evaluation projects, an attempt was made to build a taxonomy (or classification) of educational objectives. You will be familiar with biological taxonomies. These taxonomies are very helpful in communicational accuracy, better organisation and interrelation of various living things. Also in chemistry you will be familiar with classification of elements in periodic table.

The idea for developing a taxonomy or classification system was formed at an informal meeting of college examiners attending the 1948 American Psychological Association convention in Boston. After considerable discussion it was .agreed upon that a theoretical framework which could form a common frame of reference could be used for better communication among examiners. The theoretical framework might best be obtained through a, system of classifying the goals of educational process.

For developing this taxonomy certain organisational principles were developed. It was agreed that the taxonomy should be an educational-logical-psychological classification system. Thus *first* importance should be given to educational considerations. *Secondly* the taxonomy should be a logical classification for which every effort should be made to define terms as precisely as possible and to use them consistently. *Finally,* the taxonomy should be consistent with relevant and accepted psychological principles and theories, and value judgments about objectives and behaviours should be avoided.

Following this initial meeting at Boston in 1948, a series of meetings were held up till 1953 by the group of college and university examiners, where a threefold division of educational objectives was developed: *Cognitive affective* and *Psychomotor.* It was found that most of the objectives stated by teachers as well as found in the literature, could be placed rather easily in one of the three major domains or classifications. The three domains are separately discussed below.

According to (Bloom's) Taxonomy of Educational Objectives, the objectives can be classified into three domains:

1. Cognitive Domain (remembering)
2. Affective Domain (feeling)
3. Psychomotor Domain (doing)

Examples: Given below are listed some objectives of Nutrition Education in the three domains.

Cognitive Domain (Knowledge and Intellectual Skills): To help the children to:

1. understand the need for adequate food and that proper nutrition is essential for physical and mental development, health and happiness.
2. become aware of the foods available in the locality and need to produce more food,
3. become aware of the ways in which food can be prepared and make attractive, tasty and nutrition in eating.

Affective Domain (Attitude): To help the children to:

1. take interest in selecting, and in liking to eat different groups of food.
2. feel the necessity of producing more food and take interest in kitchen gardening.
3. take interest in finding out what kinds of food are available in the locality.
4. become convinced of avoiding waste of food at all levels.

Psychomotor Objective (Skill): Children:

1. select and eat proper combination of food.
2. do not eat without washing hands, but wash hands

before and after eating and develop similar hygienic food practices.

3. participate in food production at home and in school.
4. explain the kinds of food available in the locality.

THE VARIATIONS

Richard Whitfield of Faculty of Education, Cambridge has described these in the form of a summary (Fig.) showing a chain for the isolation of teaching objectives.

This summarised form will give us a clear idea of the various terms the way they are quite often used.

VARIOUS GOALS

The first two steps (Fig.) are the goals or aims; they serve to suggest general directions in which our science courses may be steered.

Justification for science in an educational setting Suggests

↓

(1) Aims for science teaching

Translation and selection gives

↓

(2) Objectives of particular courses

By selecting and relating these to specific content and teaching methods, we obtain

↓

(3) Objectives for particular lessons

Some of these at least are amenable to behavioural specification, z *e.*, identifiable in terms of observable qualities of pupils.

Fig.

1. They are general global targets (general objectives) with which we are concerned.
2. They form the basis of the general place of science in the curriculum for given groups of pupils.

Examples:

1. To develop interest of pupils in science.
2. To develop inquiring minds.
3. To help pupils to see science in relation to the rest of culture.
4. To prepare some pupils for carriers in science.
5. To help pupils to solve problems

Objectives

1. They are the more precise outcomes (specific objectives) for a particular course of teaching or even a single lesson.
2. They are derived from the aims and represent their translation into terms which are tangle in planning a course or series of lessons.
    * When objectives written in this form, they are called behavioural objectives.

Examples:

1. To develop the ability to formulate hypotheses.
2. To foster the ability to estimate experimental errors.
3. To develop skill in wiring simple circuits.
4. To increase pupils' ability to work as a term in sharing out a complex task.
5. To help pupils describe the structure of human heart.

An objective is an intent communicated by a statement describing a proposed change in a learner — a statement of what the learner is to be like when he has successfully completed a learning experience. It is a description of pattern of behaviour (performance) we want the learner to be able to demonstrate.

In the given examples of objectives some objectives can be achieved by one particular lesson and others can be achieved by many. Such objectives which are very specific in nature and can be achieved by a particular lesson are called *specific objectives*, others which will be achieved by teaching many or even the whole course are called *general objectives*.

In this way, Richard Whitfield explains that the clarification of aims and objectives is what distinguishes the 'professional' teacher from the technician carrying out someone else's orders. The discussion also shows how general aims and justifications for teaching science can be translated into more detailed statements of objectives which affect the choice of curriculum content and teaching methods.

RESULTANT OBJECTIVES

Affective domain objectives deal with interest, attitudes, values, appreciation and adjustment. These objectives describe behaviours ranging from students merely being aware that a given phenomenon exists to behaviours where they are increasingly willing to attend, respond to phenomenon with a positive feeling, attach values with it and at some point conceptualise their behaviours and feelings. Finally they organise these conceptualisations into a structure. This structure grows in complexity as it becomes his life outlook.

This shows a process by which a given phenomenon or value passed from a level of bare awareness to a position of some power to guide or control the behaviour of a person.

Affective domain objectives were further classified into five categories intended to be hierarchical in order.

Receiving (Attending): Receiving is to orient the learner to learn. This is the first step that he is willing to learn what is being given to him.

The category of receiving has three different levels, the lowest level is the awareness or being conscious of something. The next point is that he is willing to receive and then he is attentive when something is given to him.

Examples:

(i) The students are aware of scientific activities in the school.

(ii) They are willing to take part in scientific activities.

(iii) They attend activities arranged by science club.

Responding: Responding level comes after the learner has given his attention. Responding includes behaviours like compliance and willingness to respond and getting satisfaction by responding.

Examples:

(i) Students respond to the questions asked by the teacher.

(ii) Students raise hands to answer questions every time a question is asked by the teacher.

(iii) Students feel happy after answering the questions correctly.

(iv) Students take pleasure in explaining scientific phenomenon to others.

Valuing: The abstract concept is an important element of behaviour. At this level individual is not motivated by the desire to comply or obey but he is motivated because of his own valuing or assessment and commitment to the underlying value. The value system has slowly accepted and has come to be used by the student at his own criteria of worth.

Examples: Students have faith in the power of reasoning and methods of experimenting and discussions.

Organisation: When the learner develops certain values, he encounters situations for which more than one value is relevant. In such cases he is able to organise the values into a system.

Examples: Students develop a plan for doing some scientific activities and school work at home.

Characterisation by a Value or Value Complex: The individual acts constantly in accordance with the values he has developed.

Examples: Students develop a code of behaviour based on scientific attitudes.

VARIOUS PLANS

There is hardly any need today to justify the place of science in a scheme of general education for school children. Science is all pervasive. Modern societies exist on the basis of science; science is intimately related to the means of production and means of communication, including transport. Even economics and politics have to depend on scientific factors such as productivity from the land or from industry, the power of modern weapons or the speed of transportation of ground and air forces. In the present situation, therefore, anyone, in any walk of life, must be aware of a certain quantum of science and technology.

The scientific method extends far beyond science. All disciplines are becoming scientific. The method of observation, of making symbolic, graphical or linguistic models, of designing experiments, of applying reason as well as imagination to draw conclusions from data to formulate theories/ the method of keeping an objective view while theories are tested is a method which pervades every discipline. The facts of today may not be the facts of tomorrow, and theories may undergo change, but there can be no going away from the scientific method.

Science should help in reducing obscurantism and all sorts

of prejudices based on sex, caste, religion, language or region. By emphasising a rational approach science should help the development of a democratic, secular and socialist state.

The general objectives of science education have a limited utility unless they are spelt out in terms of stage-wise objectives for the guidance of educational planners, administrators, supervisors and teachers. According to Kothari Commission Report (1964-66), NCERT has laid down the following objectives as national objectives of science education in its publication, "The Curriculum for the Ten-Year School — A Framework," for various levels.

Primary (I-V): This is a very crucial stage in the life of a child. The child's spontaneity, curiosity creativity and activity in general should not be restricted by a rigid and unattractive method of teaching and environment for learning. The curriculum should take into consideration the social, intellectual, emotional and physical maturity of the child as well as the socio-economic needs of the community.

It will be helpful to identify realistically the basic minimum to be achieved in respect of each and every child and leave enough scope for individual schools to go as far beyond this basic minimum as their circumstances permit. There should be enough scope for flexibility and local adjustments. As far a number of children the primary stage may be terminal, it should be necessary to provide an education to them which prepares them for life and for self learning.

In the primary classes, the sciences should be taught as environmental studies; in Classes I and II as a composite course including both the natural and the social environment, and later on, in classes III, IV and V, as two subjects—environmental studies I (natural science) and environmental studies II (social science). One needs not lay down how much of this should be covered in a particular class. The purpose should be not to stuff the minds of children with facts and information, but to sharpen their senses, to enable them observe their environment and to enrich their experience.

Since the environment and the experiences of the children outside the school vary from place to place, the activities provided in the school should also vary so that edifice of knowledge is built not on abstract concepts but also on the solid foundations of experience drawn from the environment of the child. In such a programme a flexible syllabus should be drawn up to cater the needs of all sorts of schools. There is always a criticism that our science textbooks have generally an urban bias.

The textbook should not be given so much importance in the learning of science. What is more important at this stage is to provide teachers with guides and prepare them to develop their own instructional material. Reading materials for children should be prepared very thoughtfully so as to motivate them for reading.

The general objectives of science education at primary stage may be stated as follows.

1. The child should learn the method of inquiry in science and should begin to appreciate science and technology in everyday life,
2. The child should develop habits of cleanliness and healthful living and an understanding of the proper sanitation and hygiene of his neighbourhood.
3. The child should learn to cooperate with others and appreciate the utility of working together. Other desirable qualities of character and personality, such as initiative, leadership, honesty should be developed.
4. The child should be able to express himself freely in creative activities and should acquire habits of self-learning.

***Middle (VI-VIII)*:** At this stage the children become adolescent and this period can become difficult for many children. Problems of adjustment in the family, the school and the society begin to appear. The child becomes a boy or a girl with greater intellectual, emotional, social and physical maturity than the primary school child.

Social demands and responsibilities begin to appear. For many boys and girls, this stage is terminal after which they enter life and work. Therefore they should be prepared adequately to face life and develop capacities and attitudes for productive work in which they have to participate.

In the sciences, at this stage, physical and life sciences should be introduced. At the same time/ environmental education, nutrition, health and population education should receive adequate attention so that science is related meaningfully to life. This is the age when work experience should emphasise agricultural and technological processes and tools to help the integration of science, mathematics and technology with production and with the life of the community.

In middle classes (VI-VIII) a number of States and Union Territories have already gone ahead with the introduction of physics, chemistry and biology as disciplines. Some other States and Union Territories could develop integrated science courses upto class VIII; some could also try with groups — physical sciences (including physics and chemistry), and life sciences (including botany, zoology and human physiology).

The unit approach, which does not violate the disciplines, and actually brings them closer and provides a more logical and economical procedure, has a great potential and should be adopted. In these classes laws and theories should be gradually introduced, taking care that they are not introduced as dogmas. Pupils should be made to understand that many models are available and one of them is the one they are learning. Open-mindedness and scepticism should be encouraged.

The general objectives of science education at middle stage may be stated as follows:

1. The child should be able to apply the knowledge of science in everyday life.
2. The child should be able to investigate new knowledge in the field of science.
3. The child should develop scientific attitude.
4. The child should learn how to learn a part of scientific knowledge on his own.
5. The child should be able to solve problems around him.
6. To make the child creative.
7. To train the child in science processes.

Secondary (IX-X): The secondary stage covers the two classes, IX and X. These two classes complete the ten years of general education. After this, there are three possible courses open to students:

(i) They can enter the working force,

(ii) They can take up vocational courses, and

(iii) They can take up higher level academic courses of study to prepare for entrance to the first degree class in the college or university.

The IX and X classes may be terminal for a large majority of students who are to enter the working force. Therefore it is necessary to bring their education upto a standard which will give them the competence to enter life. The Education Commission (1964-66) had thought of a minimum national standard of attainment so that those areas of the country and those sections of the society which are backward could come up and compete fairly with the rest of the people. Thus for maintaining a continuity of the objectives of education from the previous years, it is necessary to pay attention to the academic subjects as well as to the knowledge and skill required for doing socially productive work. These two years are crucial from the-point of view of the development of the personality. While from the onset of puberty in the middle stage there are problems of adjustment which the young child has to cope with. It is at this stage that these become acute and the additional preparation for a transition from the life of a school student to that of a productive person in society has to be undertaken.

Therefore it is necessary to give the child some psychological insight into his problems and the knowledge that may help him to understand his own behaviour as well as that of others around him.

The general objectives of science education at this stage may be stated as follows:

1. The student should develop the competence to apply his knowledge to the solution of the problems around him.
2. He should have an understanding of the technological processes in agriculture and industry in use in his surroundings.
3. He should be able to contribute meaningfully to environmental conservation, the reduction of pollution, the development of proper nutrition and health and hygiene in the community.
4. He should be able to help in the development of proper habits and attitudes in the child care and in the improvement of the home.
5. He should acquire the knowledge and skills required for entry into an area of work.
6. He should learn one or two useful trades.
7. It is equally important to give him enough knowledge of the materials, tools, techniques and processes of a job family so that he can enter life with some confidence.
8. Through curricular and co-cumcular activities (science

club, science fair, science debate, science essay, science symposium, etc.) he should develop desirable scientific attitude and values like cooperation, team spirit, fellow feeling, leadership, courage, truthfulness, honesty and sincerity.

Senior Secondary (XI-XII): You will be teaching physics, chemistry or biology or just general science or integrated science. Here is a list of objectives of science teaching as identified by a group of science teachers (in a workshop at SCERT Delhi) teaching science (Physics, Chemistry or Biology) to senior secondary classes (XI-XII). Some of them may also fit in the lower classes (middle or secondary). You may or may not agree with all the objectives. You might like to add some more adjectives to this list. Thus this list of objectives of science teaching may be a guideline for you to identify some objectives which you will like to achieve at the end of your lesson, unit, course or programme. These objectives are listed below:

1. To give students up-to-date knowledge in science.
2. To develop their curiosity to learn science.
3. To train them in scientific method of learning.
4. To orient them to apply science and technology in agriculture, medicine, research and industry.
5. To develop in them the competency to apply scientific knowledge to the solution of the problems around them.
6. To enable them to contribute meaningfully to the conservation of environment, the reduction of pollution, the development of nutrition, health and hygiene conditions in the community.
7. To enable them to help in the development of proper habits and attitudes in child care and in the improvement of the home.
8. To enable them to reduce all sorts of prejudices based on sex, caste, religion, language or region.

9. To sharpen their senses to enable them to observe their environment and to enrich their experience, rather than to stuff their minds with facts and information.
10. To make them aware of these aspects of science that are environment based and life centred.
11. To train them in the use and maintenance of science equipment.
12. To make them creative.
13. To develop in them the mental faculty of open-mindedness, making them understand that there are many models of experimentation that are possible.
14. To prepare them for change and create in them confidence for facing problems of the future.
15. To enable them to formulate and test hypotheses.
16. To enable them to investigate the scientific phenomenon rather than just verifying known conclusions.
17. To enable them to investigate the scientific laws, principles and facts etc., which they can do by laboratory experiments.
18. To enable them to believe and remember scientific laws, principles, and facts etc., discovered by others and in the textbook.
19. To train them in science processes in order to discover some of the science content.
20. To involve them in learning processes as far as possible instead of treating them as passive listeners.
21. To build proper base for professional and higher science courses.

THE INTERRELATION

It is really hard to compartmentalise human behaviours clearly in terms of cognition and affect. No teacher or curriculum developer really intends one entirely without the other. There are many researches which demonstrate that cognition and affect can never be separated.

It is also noticed that the interest arises from increased information about something. According to Burner, some workers have felt that it is the process of problem solving and discovery in learning that brings about increased motivation for the subject and therefore develops interests and attitudes. Their view is that it is not much what is learned, but how it is learned which will determine the affective objectives that will be attained at the same time as the cognitive objectives.

Thus you learned about the aims and objectives of science teaching. As a science teacher you should distinguish between "aims" and "objectives" and "general and specific objectives" of science teaching. You will be teaching science at various levels — middle, secondary or senior secondary. Now you can identify objectives of science teaching at various levels. Now you know that the objectives of science teaching can be placed into three domains — cognitive, affective and psychomotor. As a teacher, for your science lessons, you can take objectives from each domain. Identify only those objectives which you feel you can achieve. They should be compatible to the cognitive level of students and the existing classroom conditions. If objectives are written in behavioural terms, teachers know what exactly they are to teach, students know what exactly they are to learn, textbook writers know what exactly they are to write and paper setters know what exactly they are to ask in examination.

PERCEIVING THE AIMS

Cognitive objectives were further classified into six categories— knowledge, comprehension, application, analysis, synthesis, and evaluation.

Knowledge: Knowledge is defined as the remembering of previously learned material. This may involve the recall of a wide range of material, from specific facts to complete theories, but all that is required is the bringing to mind of the appropriate information. Knowledge represents lowest level of learning cutcomes in the cognitive domain.

Examples: Knows common terms, knows specific facts, knows methods and procedures, knows basic concepts, knows principles, theories and structure.

Comprehension: Comprehension is defined as the ability to grasp the meaning of the material. This may be shown by *translating* material from one form to another (words to numbers), by *interpreting* material (explaining or summarising) and by establishing outcomes go one step beyond the simple remembering of material and represent the lowest level of understanding.

Examples: Understands facts and principles, interprets verbal material, interprets charts and graphs, translates verbal material to mathematical formula, estimates future consequences implied in date, justifies procedures and methods.

Application: Application refers to the ability to use learned material in new and concrete situations. This may include the application of such things as rules, methods, concepts, principles; laws and theories. Learning outcomes in this area require a higher level of understanding than those under comprehension.

Examples: Applies concepts and principles to new situations, applies laws and theories to practical situations, solves mathematical problems, constructs charts and graphs, demonstrates correct usage of a method or procedure.

Analysis: Analysis refers to the ability to breakdown material into its component parts so that its organisational structure may be understood. This may include the identification of the parts, analysis of the relationship between parts, and recognition of the organising principles involved. Learning outcomes here represent higher level of intellectual skills than comprehension and application because they require an understanding of both the content and the structural form of the material.

Examples: Recognises unstated assumptions, recognises logical fallacies in reasoning, distinguishes between facts and inferences, evaluates the relevancy of data, analyses the organisational structure of a work (art, music, writing, project report).

Synthesis: Synthesis refers to the ability to put parts together to form a new whole. This may involve the production of a unique communication (theme or speech), a plan of operation (research proposal), or a set of abstract relations (scheme for classifying information). Learning outcomes in this area stress creative behaviour, with major emphasis on the formulation of new pattern or structures.

Examples: Writes a well organised theme, gives a well organised speech, writes a creative short story (or poem or music), proposes a plan for experiment, integrates learning from different areas into a plan for solving a problem, formulates a new scheme for classifying objects (or events or ideas).

Evaluation: Evaluation is concerned with the ability to judge the value of material (statement, novel, poem, research report) for a given purpose. The judgments are to be based on definite criteria. These may be internal criteria (organisation) or external criteria (relevance to the purpose) and the student may determine the criteria. Learning outcomes in this area are highest in the cognitive hierarchy, because they contain elements of all of the other categories, plus conscious value judgments, based on clearly defined criteria.

Examples: Judges the logical consistency of written material, judges the adequacy with which conclusions are supported by data, judges the value of work (art, music, writing) by use of internal criteria, judges the value of work (art, music, writing) by use of external standards of excellence.

Five

TEACHING AIDS

MODERN DEVICES

In addition to reading, vicarious experience can be gained from still pictures, films, filmstrips, resource persons, simulations, mockups, television, and the like. The more concrete and realistic the vicarious experience, the more nearly it approaches the learning effectiveness of the first level. Of course, unless the learner realizes that he is dealing with a substitute, his learning may not be comparable to that of real-life learning.

Instructional Media: Interest in the role of the senses in learning was already there in educational circles when instructional media began their ascendancy. It has long been recognized that the various senses condition the reception of messages in the communications act. Research done by Cobun (1968) indicated that:

1 per cent of what is learned is from the sense of TASTE.

1.5 per cent of what is learned is from the sense of TOUCH.

3.5 per cent of what is learned is from the sense of SMELL.

11 per cent of what is learned is from the sense of HEARING.

83 per cent of what is learned is from the sense of SIGHT.

Retention of what is learned is likewise related to sense experience.

Observation and research by Cobun tended to show, holding time as nearly constant as possible, that people generally remember:

10 per cent of what they READ.

20 per cent of what they HEAR.

30 Per cent of what they SEE.

50 per cent of what they HEAR AND SEE.

70 per cent of what they SAY.

90 per cent of what they SAY as they do a thing.

Popular Sayings

I hear, I forget.

I see, I remember.

I do, I understand.

Characteristics

1. They should be meaningful and purposeful.
2. They should be accurate in every respect.
3. They should be simple.
4. They should be cheap.
5. As far as possible, they should be improvised.
6. They should be large enough to be properly seen by the students for whom they are meant.
7. They should be up-to date.
8. They should be easily portable.
9. They should be according to the mental level of the students.
10. They should motivate the learners.

Principles

Principle of selection: Teaching aids prove effective only when they suit the teaching objectives and unique characteristics of the special group of learners.

Following points may be kept in view in this regard:

(i) They should suit the age-level, grade-level and other characteristics of the learners.

(ii) They should have specific educational value besides being interesting and motivating.

(iii) They should be the true representatives of the real things.

(iv) They should help in the realization of desired learning objectives.

Principle of preparation: This principle requires that following points should be attended to:

(a) As far as possible, locally available material should be used in the preparation of an aid.

(b) The teachers should receive some training in the preparation of aids.

(c) The teachers themselves should prepare some of the aids.

(d) Students may be associated in the preparation of aids.

Preparation of physical control: This principle related to the arrangement of keeping aids safely and also to facilitate their lending to the teachers for use.

Principle of proper presentation: This principle implies the following points:

(i) Teachers should carefully visualise the use of teaching aids before their actual presentation.

(ii) They should fully acquaint themselves with the use

and manipulation of the aids to be shown in the classroom.

(iii) Adequate care should be taken to handle an aid in such a way as no damage is done to it.

(iv) The aid should be displayed properly so that all the students are able to see it, observe it and derive maximum benefit out of it.

(v) As far as possible, distraction of all kinds to be eliminated so that full attention may be paid to the aid.

Principle of response: This principle demands that the teachers guide the students to respond actively to the audio-visual stimuli so that they derive the maximum benefit in learning.

Principle of evaluation: This principle stipulates that there should be continuous evaluation of both the audio-visual material and accompanying techniques in the light of the realisation of the desired objectives.

Problems: While all these aids are becoming more and more popular day by day, there are still some problems to be faced and solved. These are:

Apathy of the teachers: Teachers in general are yet to be convinced that teaching with words alone is very tedious, wasteful and ineffective.

Indifference of students: The judicious use of aids arouses interest but when used without a definite purpose they lose their significance and importance.

Ineffectiveness of the aids: Due to the absence of proper planning and the lethargy of the teacher and without proper preparation, correct presentation, application and discussion and the essential follow-up work, the aids do not prove their full usefulness. A film like a good lesson has various steps—Preparation, Presentation, Application and Discussion.

Financial hurdles: The Central and State Governments have set up Boards of Audio-Visual Education and have chalked out interesting programmes for the popularization of teaching aids but the lack of finances is not enabling them to do their best.

Absence of electricity: Most of the Projectors, Radio and TV cannot work without the electric current which is not available in a large number of schools.

Lack of facilities for training: Training colleges or specialised agencies should make special provision to train teachers and workers in the use of these aids.

Coordination between Centre and States: Good film libraries, museums of audio-visual provision to train teachers and workers in the use of these aids.

Language difficulty: Most educational films are in English. We should have these in Hindi and other important Indian languages.

Not catering to local needs: Little attention is paid in the production of audio-visual aids to the local sociological, psychological and pedagogical factors.

Improper selection of films: Films are not selected according to the classroom needs.

The future: Today, the problem is not whether visual aids should have a place in education. Their place has been recognised long ago.

The problem, now, is that of extending the benefits of these aids to all teachers and all children. The future can be bright if there is proper planning on the part of the Government and coordination between producers, teachers and students.

Useful and effective aids can be produced after getting the reaction of the audience and doing research work in the field. A great deal is being done already but a lot more still remains to be done.

THE DIVISION

Classification Number 1: Projected and Non-Projected Aids

Projected Aids	*Graphic Aids*	*Display Boards*	*3-Dimensional Aids*	*Audio Aids*	*Activity Aids*
1. Films	1. Cartoons	Blackboard	Diagrams	Radio	1. Computer-Assisted Instruction
2. Filmstrips	2. Charts	Bulletin	Models	Recordings	2. Demonstrations
3. Opaque Projector	3. Comics	Flannel Board	Mockups	Television	3. Dramatics
4. Overhead Projector	4. Diagrams	Magnetic Board	Objects		4. Experimentation
5. Slides	5. Flash Cards	Peg Board	Puppets		5. Field Trips
	6. Graphs		Specimens		6. Programmed Instruction
	7. Maps				7. Teaching Machines
	8. Photographs				
	9. Pictures				
	10. Posters				

Classification Number 2: Audio Materials, Visual Materials And Audio-Visual Materials

Audio Materials	*Visual Materials*	*Audio-visual Materials*
(1) Language Laboratories	(1) Bulletin boards	(1) Demonstrations
(2) Radio	(2) Chalk boards	(2) Films
(3) Sound distribution system sets	(3) Charts	(3) Printed materials with recorded sound
(4) Tape and disco recordings	(4) Drawings etc.	(4) Sound filmstrips
	(5) Exhibits	(5) Study trips
	(6) Film strips	(6) Television
	(7) Flash cards	(7) Videotapes
	(8) Flannel boards	
	(9) Flip books	
	(10) Illustrated books	
	(11) Magnetic boards	

Contd...

Audio Materials	*Visual Materials*	*Audio-visual Materials*
	(12) Maps	
	(13) Models	
	(14) Pictures	
	(15) Posters	
	(16) Photographs	
	(17) Self-instructional	
	(18) Silent films	
	(19) Slides	

Classification Number 3: Big Media and Little Media

Big media include computer, VCR and TV. Little media include radio, films strips, graphic, audio cassettes and various visuals.

Classification Number 4: Three Dimensional Aids

(i) Models

(ii) Mock-ups

(iii) Specimens.

Three dimensional aids are the replicas or substitutes of real objects.

All the learning experiences which can be utilised for classroom teaching are shown by Edgar Dale in a pictorial device—'pinnacle form'—which he called the 'cone of experience'. If we go up the pinnacle from its base, we find that every aid has been arranged in the order of increasing abstractness or decreasing directness. In a simple language, it may be stated that the 'cone' classifies the audiovisual aids according to their effectiveness in communication—aid at the base of the cone as 'most effective'—relative effect gradually decreases.

At the pinnacle of the 'Cone', the direct, purposeful experiences are represented. At the pinnacle of the 'Cone', the verbal symbols are represented.

The experiences included in the cone are as indicated below:

Direct, purposeful experience: The experiences gained through the senses are direct and purposeful. It has been amply observed, "An ounce of experience is better than a tonne of theory, simply because it is only as an experience that any theory has vital and verifiable significance." This, direct experience is gained through the aids mentioned at the base of the cone.

Contrived experience: When the real thing cannot be perceived directly, its simplification becomes necessary. Contrived experience is like a working model which is an editing of reality and differs from the original either in size or in complexity. The real object may be too small or too big, may be confused or concealed. In such a situation imitation is preferred for better and easier understanding.

Dramatic participation: In dramatics, certain real events are presented through the play, the pageant (kind of community drama, usually based on local history), pantomine (actors do not speak, make movements), tablean (pictureline scene in which the characteristics stand still, silently), and the puppets.

THE ILLUSTRATION

Actual objects: Actual objects and specimens are indispensable in science and other subjects. They are very vivid and impressive. They make a direct appeal to the senses of children. It is not possible for a child to have a clear picture of a river, a factory or a mountain unless he has seen these. The teaching of history and geography can never be effective without visiting places of importance, valleys, lakes, old forts, monuments, etc.

The students get a correct idea of various minerals when they are shown these objects. In framing the multiplication table, counting of beads and sticks prove to be very useful at the earlier stages.

Blackboard: Blackboard and a piece of chalk prove very helpful in illustrating concepts and ideas to the students. These can be used for drawing diagrams and sketches, etc. Blackboard is a simple and unique device which, in spite of new devices and techniques in teaching, is irreplacable as well as indispensable. It is the oldest and the best friend of a teacher. It is the mirror through which students visualise all about the teacher's mind regarding the lesson in hand, his way of explaining, illustrating and teaching as a whole. It is the cheapest teaching device and continues to be the '*sine quo non*' of our educational system. It is the most universally used aid. Writing on clay and sand was the ancient form of blackboard writing. It helps 'crystallizing' the main points, 'summarising' and 'reviewing'.

Blackboard

1. The teacher can illustrate the main points of the lesson on the blackboard.
2. Abstract statements can be clarified in the exposition stage and a summary containing the salient features can be given at the recapitulatory stage.
3. Questions and problems can be listed on the blackboard.
4. Pupils' interest in classwork can be stimulated by blackboard writings and drawings.
5. A teacher can use the blackboard for graphs, graphics, sketches, maps and statistics, etc.
6. A blackboard provides a lot of scope for creative and decorative work.
7. The teacher can erase writings and drawings and start afresh.
8. It helps the teacher to focus the attention of his students on the lesson. It takes heed of varying capacities and rates of grasp of the students.
9. A teacher can review the whole lesson for the benefit of the class with the help of the blackboard.

Types of Blackboards

Fixed blackboard: Fixed in the wall facing the class and normally made of wood or concrete cement.

Blackboard on easel: A portable and adjustable blackboard put on a wooden easel can be taken out of the classroom while taking classes in the open.

Roller blackboard: Made of thick canvas wrapped on a roller mostly used for teaching higher classes.

Graphic board: It has graphic lines and is used for teaching mathematics, science and statistics.

Magna board: A board which enables teachers to make three-dimensional demonstrations with objects on a vertical surface. Small magnets are used to hold suitable objects fixed wherever they are put on this vertical surface.

Chalk Boards of Different Types of Surfaces

1. Paint-coated pressed wood.
2. Dull finished plastic surface.
3. Vitreous-coated steel surface.
4. Ground glass board.

Chalks

Colour of the blackboard	*Colour of the chalk*
1. Green chalk board	White or Yellow chalk
2. Grey board	Yellow
3. Red chalk board	Green, Yellow
4. Orange chalk board	Blue or light Green
5. Yellow chalk board	Blue
6. Rose chalk board	Purple, dark Blue
7. Black chalk board	Any colour

Effective Use of Blackboard

Following points may be kept in view while using the blackboard:

1. Blackboard should be kept clean so-that writing on it could be easily read by the students from all parts of the room.
2. Writing on the blackboard should be legible.
3. Letters and drawings should be large enough to be seen from all parts of the room.
4. Writing should be started from the top left corner.
5. Writing should be in straight rows.
6. Extreme lower corner of the blackboard should not be made use of as writing on it cannot be seen easily.
7. Material on the blackboard should not be covered by standing.
8. Only salient points of the subject-matter should be written on the blackboard.
9. Diagrammatic visual presentation involving many processes should be prepared before the beginning of the lesson.
10. It should be ensured that blackboard is well lighted by natural or artificial means.
11. Everything needed for the blackboard should be got together before the class begins *i,e.,* collection of chalk, rulers, T. Square, Compass, Projector, etc.
12. While writing on the blackboard, the teacher should ensure that the class is attentive.
13. Duster and not hand or handkerchief should be used in cleaning the blackboard.
14. Occasionally students may be asked to write or draw diagram on the blackboard.
15. Teachers should develop the ability to draw freely on

the blackboard. The map or chart or diagram that grows before the very eyes of the students is much more useful and valuable than a well finished map, chart or diagram.

16. It should be ensured that the blackboard is periodically serviced.

Charts: A chart is a combination of pictorial, graphic, numerical or vertical material which presents a clear visual summary. The most commonly used types of charts include outline charts, tabular charts, flow charts and organisation charts. Other types of charts are technical diagrams and process diagrams. Flip charts and flow charts are also being used. Ready made charts are available for use in teaching in almost all areas in all subjects. But charts prepared by a teacher himself incorporating his own ideas and lines of approach of the specific topic are more useful.

Purposes of Charts

Charts serve the following purposes:

1. For showing relationship by means of facts, figures and statistics.
2. For presenting materials symbolically.
3. For summarising information.
4. For showing continuity in process.
5. For presenting abstract ideas in visual form.
6. For showing development of structure.
7. For creating problems and stimulating thinking.
8. For encouraging utilisation of other media of communication.
9. For motivating the students.

How to use Charts Effectively?

1. Teacher-made charts should be preferred.

2. Students should be involved in the preparation of charts.
3. Charts should be so large that every detail depicted should be visible to every pupil in the class wherever he is sitting.
4. Charts should display information only about one specific area in a subject.
5. A chart should not contain too much written material.
6. A chart should not contain too many details.
7. A chart should give a neat appearance.
8. When a chart is to be used in the classroom, the teacher should make sure that there is provision for hanging the chart at a vantage point.
9. The teacher should have a pointer to point out specific factors in the chart.
10. Straight pins, staples, pegboard lips, gummed hangers, paper-clips, folded making tapes may all be used for fastening charts without damaging them.
11. Charts should be carefully stored and preserved for use in future.

Types of Charts

The following is a list of basic types of charts in terms of arrangements and the kinds of ideas which they may express:

1. The narrative chart, an extended left-to-right arrangement of facts and ideas for expressing: *(a)* The events in a process such as shoe making, oil cracking, or the like, *(b)* The events in the development of a significant issue to its point of resolution or to present status (sometimes a time limit). Example: the events leading to the separation of the Bangladesh from Pakistan, the events leading to the establishment of the idea that an individual should be free and that he should have a voice in his own government and the

events leading to increased regulation of business by government, *(c)* Technological improvement over a period of years such as improvement in transportation, communication, manufacturing etc.

2. The tabulation chart, a left-to-right, top-to-bottom arrangement of facts and ideas for expression: *(a)* Numerical data for making comparisons, *(b)* Lists products, mountains, rivers, or the like in selected areas.
3. The cause and effect chart, usually a limited left-to-right arrangement of facts and ideas for expressing: (a) Relationship between standard of living and such factors as economic system, availability of natural resources, level of technological advancement, (b) Relationship between a culture and neighbouring cultures, (c) Relationship between rights and responsibilities, (d) Relationship between a complex of conditions and change or conflict, (e) Relationship - between the elected and the electors, (f) Relationship between community workers and the community which supports them.
4. The chain charts, a circular or semi-circular arrangement of facts and ideas for expressing: *(a)* Transitions, such as the transition from raw materials to useful products, *(b)* Cycles, such as the water cycle.
5. The evolution chart, a left-to right arrangement of facts and ideas for expressing: (a) Changes in specific item from beginning to date, perhaps with projections into the future. Example: origin of the automobile and its subsequent development, early basic homes and changes in basic homes to date, (b) Change in standard in food consumption, length of work, weak purchasing power of a rupee, or the like.

Diagrams: Diagrams are very helpful in supplementing vertical illustrations in teaching. Difficult operations may be explained with the help of diagrams. The parts of a flower or leaf can be suitably explained by means of sketches drawn by the teacher in front of the class on the blackboard: Simple diagrams can be used to explain different phenomena in geography and science. The diagrams of battle plans and forts can be drawn on the blackboard. The area and volume, etc., in mathematics can be illustrated through diagrams. A teacher is expected to possess the skill of drawing diagrams easily, neatly, rapidly and readily on the blackboard.

Epidiascope: The epidiascope is an instrument which can project images or printed matter or small opaque objects on a screen, or it can project images of a 4" × 4" slide. With the help of any epidiascope, any chart, diagram, map, photograph and picture can be projected on the screen without tearing it off from the book.

No slide is needed for this purpose. An epidiascope serves two purposes. It works as epidiascope when it is used to project an opaque object. It works as epidiascope when it is used to project slides (by operating a lever). It works on the principle of horizontal straight line projection with a lamp, plane mirror and projection lens. A strong light from the lamp falls on the opaque object. A plane mirror placed at an angle of 45° over the project, reflects the light so that it passes through the projection lens forming a magnified image on the screen.

Film Strip: A film strip is 35 mm wide and has a series of 12 to 48 picture frames arranged in a sequence so that they develop a theme. A film strip can be prepared by taking a series of photographs using a 35 mm camera and then by taking a positive print of the negative film on another 35 mm film.

Globe: Knowledge of map is unreal without the knowledge of globe-the true map. It is the true representative of earth's physical personality. A globe gives a true idea of the total environment at a glance in a classroom situation. It is through globe that a child can understand the concepts of time, space, wind's planetary relations and proportion. Hence, every school shall have globes. Four types of globes may be kept in every school. (1) Political globes, (2) Physical globes, (3) Washable projection globes, (4) Celestial globes.

Graphs: Graphs are flat pictures which employ dots, lines or pictures to visualise numerical and statistical data to show relationships or statistics.

Several Types of Graphs

Line graph: In a line graph, data is represented with the help of simple lines horizontally or vertically drawn. For increasing the interest and readability of concepts, pictorial illustrations and cartoons are occasionally used on the line graph.

Bar graph: A bar graph consists of bars arranged, horizontally or vertically from a 'zero' base. The colour, length and size of the bars represent different values.

Circle graph: Data may be presented in a circle graph.

Magic lantern: Magic lantern is the earliest invention in the history of audio-visual aids used for projecting pictures from a transparency (slide) on a wall or screen. When the figure or illustration is very small and it is required to be shown to the entire class, a transparent slide of the small figure is prepared. Then, this slide is placed into the slide carrier part of the magic lantern. This magic lantern device projects it on the screen by enlarging its dimension and making the vision more clear and sharp

Map Study

Significance of map study: In several subjects, especially social studies, the learning of many geographical, historical and economic concepts remains unreal, inadequate and incomplete without map media. A resourceful teacher by motivating the pupils will turn the fear of map into the genuine love for them. This, however, presupposes the invariable uses of maps at every possible opportunity by the teacher in the classroom, and the possession of individual atlases by the pupils. Every student should also know certain elementary aspects of map preparation such as copying, enlarging and reducing, symbolizing, colouring, and preparation of key. Most of the students develop an aversion to maps because they do not know skills relating to map preparation.

Meaning of map: A map is an accurate representation of plain surface in the form of a diagram drawn to scale, the details of boundaries of continents, countries, of etc. Geographical details like location of mountains, rivers, altitude of a place, contours of the earth surface and important' locations can also be represented accurately with reference to a convenient scale with suitable colour scheme.

Identification of Various Aspects of Maps

1. Understanding and interpreting the key of index.
2. Understanding the lines-boundary lines, lines of communication, lines indicating the rivers, contours, meridians and parallels.
3. Understanding the colours, tints, shadows, symbols in a map or globe.
4. The top of every map is not north, but the direction of northern pole is north.
5. Distinction between the various types of maps such as relief, political, distribution maps, etc.
6. Understanding of the position of earth in the universe. Many students suffer from a notion that the earth leans in June towards the Sun northwards and in December southwards and thus the seasons are formed. Earth never dances that way. The student shall understand that the inclination of earth is constant and the learning effect changes due to its rotation around the sun.

Various Types of Maps

Relief maps (regional and the world): This requires the knowledge of colours, contours, symbols and the other connected ethics of map making.

Historical maps: Maps in history reveal the changing times and the growth and decline of various kingdoms. Knowledge of lines of boundaries and other symbols is necessary.

Distribution maps: Generally, the student shall associate with the following types of distribution maps: (1) Vegetation maps, (2) Population maps, (3) Economic maps, (4) Statistical maps, (5) Dot maps, (6) Pictorial maps, (7) Language, race and other human division maps, etc.

Geographical maps: Contour maps, weather maps, seismological maps, archaeological maps, rainfall maps, geological maps, etc.

Microfilm: The microfilm and microfiche are used widely for storage and retrieval of information. Microfilms contain photographed reading material on 35 mm film, each frame being the reduced photograph of a printed page. Thus, printed matter of a book can be stored in *a* small loop of 35 mm film. When the microfilm is passed through *a* microfilm reader, an enlarged image approximately of the size of the printed page is formed on a ground glass (rear-view) screen and the observer can read the matter. By moving the film through the microfilm reader, images of different pages can be obtained and read.

Models: Models are substitutes for real things. A model is a three-dimensional representation of a real thing. Models are concrete objects to explain clearly the structure or functions of real things. A model is a replica of the original. Models enable students to have a correct concept of the object. Being three dimensional, models evoke great interest and simplify matters. Models enable us to reduce or enlarge objects to an observable size. It may not be possible or even practicable to make students see the whole of a large industrial unit or even a large machine unit, but a model will give the correct perspective. Preparation of models could, form a topic for project work. It is essential to create interest in creative activity in students. Models are working as well as static. A working model will secure immediate attention and serve as motivation to learn. Model can be prepared with several kinds of materials like cardboard, plastic, plaster of paris, wood, clay, and thermocol etc.

Museum: The Secondary Education Commission, on the role of school museums observed, "Museums play a great part in the education of school children as they bring home to them much more vividly than any prosaic lectures, the discoveries of the past and the various developments that have taken place in many fields of science and technology." Again the Commission observes, "We believe it is necessary from the educational point of view to establish such museums in important centres at least wherein both ancient and modern collections will be exhibited and in some cases even demonstrations given of the actual process of development of various scientific discoveries. Nothing can impress students in the formative age so much as the actual visualising of these experiments in a graphic manner,"

Museums are made up of materials used in classroom teaching which, in many cases, are collected, classified and exhibited by students, with or without the help of a teacher. The museum activities may be an extracurricular function of the class or the school or they may be incorporated into a scientific-experimental method of teaching. The objectives of this type of museum are:

(a) to form within the school or the classroom an embryonic community dedicated to the usual occupations reflected in the school life of adults;

(b) to permit visual instruction and experimentation with actual museum specimens;

(c) to stimulate enthusiasm for study and research among both teachers and students;

(d) to stimulate interest, cooperation and participation in the cultural activities and scientific research conducted by the larger museums;

(e) to instruct students in proper scientific methods of laboratory, research and museum conservation and exhibition techniques;

(f) to form, in the absence of larger museums in the community, a nucleus from which the classroom museum can grow beyond the limits of the school to serve ultimately the community and the region as a whole.

Exhibit programmes, interpretation, visual communication: What then are some of the ways in which museums as cultural and educational centres of the community can communicate successfully with their transitory visitors of heterogeneous composition? Based on various audience-testing experiments the following media can be used to heighten the effectiveness of visual communication.

- ***Dramatic labels:*** Usually they are far too short in the museums or far too long. They actually frighten away rather than entice the average museum visitor. Experiments suggest that large letters placed at the focal point of the case or exhibit area will successfully headline the exhibit and catch the visitor's attention. Like a newspaper headline, the main label tends to direct the eye to smaller, less conspicuous letters that outline the most important points of the exhibit.

Dramatic lighting: Light is a means of visual communication as well as an attention getter. Coloured lights that change, fade or highlight an exhibit can be used with great dramatic effect. Light can also be used to tell a story and to convey a sense of passing time. Light is particularly important in art museums.

Dramatic utilization: Again experiments suggest that museum visitors should be given a chance to touch exhibits as well as to see them. Of course, much depends on the nature and expendability of the object involved but certain types of material-objects of wood, stone and metal and special "touch me" samples of animal skins and fabrics-can be used with great success to satisfy the visitor's urge to which while permitting a minimum of danger.

Dramatic sound effects: Sound, like light, can be used to heighten the dramatic effect of visual communication. For example, an Amazon rain forest exhibition can be made vastly more effective by adding the sound of tropical rain, the croaking of frogs, the chattering of monkeys, and the beat of drums. An exhibit of mediaeval art can be made more meaningful if it is accompanied by music of the same period:

Effective use of space: Special concepts are also important in planning visitor traffic patterns within the exhibit areas.

Pictures: Pictures are very much liked by children and especially of lower classes, pictures provide an environment of 'reality'. A lesson in history can be made interesting and stimulating by showing the pictures of Kings and queens, costumes and dresses, forts and weapons, monuments and tombs, etc. Similarly in a geography lesson, we can show the pictures of animals, deserts, lakes, mountains and rivers, etc., and also the various aspects of lives of people of other lands with great effect.

Following points need to be kept in view while showing pictures to the students:

1. Child's point of view should be the main criterion in the selection of pictures.
2. Pictures should be relevant to the topic.
3. As far as possible, pictures may be coloured.
4. Pictures should be accurate and of a suitable size.

5. It is desirable if the teacher himself prepares the pictures and takes help from the students.
6. Pictures should be shown in such a way that all students in the class can easily watch.
7. Too many pictures should not be displayed in one lesson.
8. After showing the picture, it should be removed from the view of the students.
9. Sufficient time should be given to see the picture.
10. Students who are good at drawing should be encouraged to draw pictures.

Projector

Micro-projector: The combination of a microscope and a slide projector is an instrument called micro-projector. The microscope is used to see very minute parts of objects by magnifying the same hundreds of times. The minute part usually of a plant or an animal is put on a glass slide and a magnified image formed by a combination of leuses in a microscope which can be seen by an individual through the naked eye. The micro-projector attachment consists of a projection lens; a plane mirror fixed at 45 degrees to the vertical plane and a vertical ground glass screen. It is very useful in teaching science.

Overhead projector (OHP): Over head projector is a device that can project a chart, a diagram, a map, a table or for that matter, anything written on transparent plates, upon a screen or the white wall before students in a class. This makes teaching illuminative, illustrative and impressive. It also saves a great deal of the teacher's time used in drawing or writing. These transparencies can also be preserved by the teacher for future display while taking up the same topic. It is very simple to prepare such transparencies. All that a teacher has to do is to draw or write, as the case may be, upon transparent plates with any dark ink with a fibre tipped pen. Any material meant for display before the class while teaching can also be typed on such transparencies using a good carbon paper. In case transparencies are to be washed out for use, washable water colour can also be used for writing on the transparencies.

Slide projector: With a slide projector, photographic slides can be projected on the screen or the wall before the class. Photographs of relevant matter meant for teaching in the class can be developed on celluloid slides and displayed with the help of such a projector. The teacher's lesson can also be recorded on an audio cassette and played with a tape recorder suitably synchronising with the slides by manipulating a remote control switch. Such an arrangement is called a tape-slide sequence. In case there are several slides to be shown in quick succession, the tape-slide sequence can bring as interesting an effect on the viewers as do the movie films. An ordinary slide projector has a frame containing two slits into which slides are put for focusing. They are manually and continuously replaced by other slides one after another. An improved type of a slide projector consists of a circular disc with more slits where even a hundred or more slides can be inserted in a sequential order which can be projected on the screen with the help of a remote control switch to be suitably manipulated by the teacher as he delivers the lesson.

Puppets: Puppetry is one of the old and popular arts in India. The use of puppets has been very popular in China, Egypt, Greece and Japan. Puppets can serve as an effective aid to learning. They can be made to illustrate lessons in civics, geography, history and hygiene. Puppets throw a lot of light in an interesting way on the life of historical personages if they are accompanied by effective narration. There should be plenty of dancing and music in the display of puppetry. While presenting puppet programmes, the age and tastes of the pupils should be duly considered. A short puppet play is always preferable to a long play. Puppets are of three types: (i) Hand puppets which fit in the hand like a glove and are operated from below by fingers. (i) Rod puppets which are operated from below the stage by a combination of rods and springs, (iii) Marionettes or string puppets which are figures with moving limbs. These are operated from the above by means of strings.

Reprographic equipment: Reprographic is a branch of technology dealing with methods of duplication or reproduction. Duplication involves making a number of identical copies of the original. Reproduction enables preparation of one or more identical copies of the original, same size or of different size in monochrome or colour. Equipment and processes, included are: duplicators, reflex printing and photography.

Record player: Record players are a means of audio playback. They are older types of hardware using records of discs for the needed playback. Four sizes of records 7", 10", 12" and 16" are in common use. There are also high speed record player with standard stylus. The record players now in use are equipped with speed changer mechanisms permitting the playing of the slower long-playing 45, 33⅓ and 16⅔ r.p.m. records played by microgrove stylus.

The use of recorded pieces in education has great value in language learning, appreciation of poetry and literature and presentation of brief dramatised episodes from history, from development of musical knowledge and discrimination. Long-playing records with 20 minutes of recorded information per side provide several diverse selections inscribed on each side and are very suitable for classroom instructional purposes. The needed selection for a particular learning situation can be easily identified by the specific microgrove ring it occupies on the record. 'Talking books' for the blind also consists of recordings of essential literature for the visually handicapped. The older, manually wound spring powered gramophone's place now has been taken up by electrically powered multi-speed record players and changers with built-in amplifying unit or linked to separate amplifying units and speakers. Likewise, the older mechanical recording has given place to electrical imprinting involving greater clarity and fidelity.

Tape-recorder: A tape-recorder in its own can be very effective for classroom instruction. Pre-recorded tapes consisting of lessons by eminent teachers on any subject can be played in the class. Such instructions become impressive not only because of the novelty but also because of their being well-thought out and planned. The tape-recorder has proved to be a boon in teaching foreign languages like English. Pre-recorded tapes on English lessons can be played in the classroom to teach not only the contents of the lesson but also proper accent, pronunciation and intonation which an average English teacher very much lacks.

Video tapes played through TV: Pre-recorded video tapes can be played through TV in the classroom. Video films on educational topics shown through TV in the classroom have the same effect on the students as the ordinary cinematic educational films do. Video films have the added advantage over ordinary films in that the arrangement is compact and requires little space and time for manipulation. It is the most convenient of all audio-visual teaching-learning materials.

Video cassettes: The potential advantage of video cassette lies in the fact that control of the equipment and the learning process is placed in the hands of the learner through control over the mechanics of the machine, i.e. stopping, starting, timing, reviewing and previewing and consequently the capacity to order the sequence of events, controls the rate of learning, and facilitates practice sequences.

The potential exists for providing the basis for learning a wide range of motor, intellectual and cognitive and interpersonal skills, as well as affective aspects. These are important aspects which printed materials cannot deal with adequately.

This facility could be particularly useful where distance education programmes are involved with updating skills and techniques of workers in the field.

For example, new horticulture techniques can be transmitted to field workers to improve farming techniques. Mid-career retraining can also be catered for.

In some countries as a way of regionalizing a centrally produced programme, video cassette programmes are being built round the study centre concept, a location where several video machines are available to which students bring their study notes. The students run the programmes as individuals. Sometimes study centres provide for group sessions during which video cassettes are played. Unless some supplementary teaching is provided, this technique can become another version of broadcast technology.

In other countries some institutions assume that students can gain access to such equipment and make programmes which will be used on an individual basis as either supplementary learning material or integral to the teaching programme.

The problems associated with video cassettes are of two kinds: (i) cost; and (ii) production of programmes.

(i) Equipment costs cannot always be kept down by using lower quality equipment. Cheaper equipment formats do not enable technical material such as animal or plant tissue to be represented adequately or tapes to be reproduced in quantity without loss of fidelity.

(ii) Video production for educational purposes calls for new techniques different from the entertainment modes. Producers, directors, scriptwriters need to be knowledgeable about teaching and learning. Many of the old techniques of film and television will no longer be of use. For example, the very basic concept that programmes must have a beginning, a middle, and an end will no longer apply as a cassette could just as easily consist of a series of short video events which sets a problem, teaches a technique, or brings together a range of visual material to make concepts or principles clear.

MULTI-DIMENSIONAL AIDS

Three dimensional aids serve as good substitutes for the real objects. There is no doubt that an encounter with real objects serves as an unmatchable source of learning. But on account of several reasons it may not be possible to bring the real objects in the classroom. The real objects may be too large to move or store in the classroom. It may be too small to be seen for a group of students. It can be too complicated in real form to be understood. Its movements may be too slow to be studied completely. It can be too expensive to be purchased by an educational institution. Being handicapped in such situations, a teacher has to search for some good substitute for the real objects.

Models diagrams, mock-ups and specimens are the important three dimensional aids.

Models: Models are the replicas or copies of the real objects. Models are usually of three types: solid, cross-sectional and working. Models are concrete objects, some considerably larger than the real object. Sectional models explain clearly the structure or functions of the original. In some cases working models of the original are used where the specific function of the original is duplicated and could be explained easily.

Following are the important functions of models:

1. Models simplify reality.
2. Models concretise abstract concepts.

3. Models enable us to reduce or enlarge objects to an observable size.
4. A model provides the correct concept of an industrial unit or a bridge or a dam like, the Bhakra Dam etc.
5. A working model explains the various processes of objects and machines.
6. Preparation of models could form a topic for project work. This is very helpful to create interest in creative activity in pupils.

Cardboard, plastic, plaster of paris, wood thermocol' and metal, etc., can be used in the preparation of a model.

Mock-ups: A mock-up refers to a specialised model or working replica of the object being depicted. In a mock-up, a certain element of the original reality is emphasised or highlighted to make it more meaningful for the purpose of instruction. While a model is a recognizable limitation of an object (though larger or smaller than the original one), a mock-up may or may not be similar in appearance. Mock-ups of aeroplanes, automobile engines, bridges, ships and tunnels, etc., may be demonstrated for explaining their structure and actual working. Mock-ups are often used in technical institutions for training purposes.

Dioramas: A diorama is a three dimensional scene in depth incorporating a group of modelled objects and figures in a natural setting. The diorama scene is set up on a small stage with a group of modelled objects kept on the foreground which is blended into a painted realistic background. Dioramas are very effective in the teaching of biological and social sciences.

DEFINITION AND SIGNIFICANCE

Audio-Visual aids, audio-visual material, audio-visual media, communication technology, educational or instructional media and learning resources — all these terms, broadly speaking, mean the same thing. Earlier the term used was audio-visual aids in education. With the advancement in the means of communication and that of technology, educators coined new terms, More specifically media refers to films, filmstrips, recordings, etc. The use of newer terms Educational Technology or Instructional Technology is primarily due to the dynamic expansion of programmed learning, computer assisted instruction and education T.V. This revolution in the field of audio-visual education is the outcome of the development in electronics, notably those involving the radio, tape recorder and computer.

Brief history of the use of audio-visual aids: A Dutch humanist, theologian and writer Desiderious Erasmus (1466-1536) discouraged memorization as a technique of learning and advocated that children should learn through the aid of pictures or other visuals. John Amos Comenius (1592-1670) prepared a book known as *Orbis Sensulium Pictus.* (The world of Sense Objects) which contained about 150 pictures on aspects of everyday life. The book is considered to be the first illustrated textbook for childhood education.

This book gained wide publicity and was used in childhood education centres all over the world. Jean Jacques Rousseau (1712-1778) and other educators stressed the need of pictures and other play materials. Rousseau condemned the use of words by teachers and he stressed 'things'. He pleaded that the teaching process must be directed to the learner's natural curiosity. Pestalozzi (1756-1827) put Rousseau's theory into action in his 'object method'. He based instruction on sense perception. The term 'Visual education' was used as early as 1926 by Lelson I.Green.

Eric Ashby (1967) identified four revolutions in education: education from home to school, written words as tool of education, invention of printing and use of books and lastly the fourth revolution in the use of electronic media i.e., radio, television, tape recorder and computer in education.

Burton: Audio-visual aids are those sensory objects or images which initiate or stimulate and reinforce learning.

Carter V. Good: audio-visual aids are those aids which help in completing the triangular process of learning i.e., motivation, classification and stimulation.

Edgar Dale: Audio-visual are those devices by the use of which communication of ideas between persons and groups in various teaching and training situations is helped. These are also termed as multisensory materials.

Good's dictionary of education: Audio-visual aids are anything by means of which learning process may be encouraged or carried on through the sense of hearing or sense of sight.

Kinder, S. James: Audio-visual aids are any device which can be used to make the learning experience more concrete, more realistic and more dynamic.

Mckown and Roberts: Audio-visual aids are supplementary devices by which the teacher, through the utilization of more than one sensory channels is able to clarify, establish and correlate concepts, interpretations and appreciations.

THE IMPORTANCE

Audio-visual aids or devices or technological media or learning devices are added devices that help the teacher to clarify, establish, co-relate and coordinate accurate concepts, interpretations and appreciations and enable him to make learning more concrete, effective, interesting, inspirational, meaningful and vivid. They help in completing the triangular process of learning viz., motivation-clarification-stimulation. The aim of teaching with technological media is 'clearing the channel between the learner and the things that are worth learning'. The basic assumption underlying Audio-visual Aids is that learning—clear understanding—stems from sense experience. The teacher must 'show' as well as 'tell'.

Audio-visual aids provide significant gains in informational learning, retention and recall, thinking and reasoning, activity, interest, imagination, better assimilation and personal growth and development. The aids are the stimuli for learning 'why', 'how', 'when' and 'where'. The 'hard to understand principles' are usually made clear by the intelligent use of skilfully designed instructional aids.

According to Gandhiji, "True education of the intellect can only come through a proper exercise and training of bodily organs—hands, feet, eyes, ears and nose."

Commenting on the use of audio-visual aids, the Kothari Commission 1964-66 observed that it should indeed bring about an 'educational revolution' in the country. It further stated that the supply of teaching aids to every school was essential for the improvement of the quality of teaching.

The National Policy of Education, 1986 and as modified in 1992 has laid a great stress on the use of teaching aids, especially improvised aids, to make teaching-learning more effective and realistic.

In the words of Edgar Dale, "Because audio-visual materials supply concrete basis for conceptual thinking, they give rise to meaningful concepts enriched by meaningful association, hence they offer the best antidote for the disease of verbalism."

Some of the important values of the proper use of audio-visual aids are given below:

Antidote to the disease of verbal instruction: They help to reduce verbalism. They help in giving clear concepts and thus help to bring accuracy in learning. As observed by Raymound Wyman (1957) "We (teacher) tell students, and we provide them with written material so much of the time. Words are wonderful. They are easily produced, reproduced, stored and transported. But the overuse or excessive use of words can result in serious problem, chiefly, the problem of verbalism (using or adopting words or phrases without considering what they mean) and forgetting."

Best motivation: They are the best motivators. The students work with more interest and zeal. They are more attentive.

Clear images: Clear images are formed when we see, hear, touch, taste and smell as our experiences are direct, concrete and more or less permanent. Learning through the senses becomes the most natural and consequently the easiest.

Vicarious experience: It is beyond doubt that the first-hand experience is the best type of educative experience. But it is neither practicable nor desirable to provide such experience to pupils. Substituted experiences may be provided under such conditions. There are many inaccessible objects and phenomena. For example, it is not possible for the pupils living in India to see the Eskimoe. Similarly, it is not possible for an average man to climb the Mount Everest. There are innumerable such things to which it is not possible to have direct access. So, in all such cases, these aids help us.

Variety: 'Mere chalk and talk' do not help. Audio-visual aids give variety and provide different tools in the hands of the teacher.

Freedom: When audio-visual aids are employed, there is great scope for children to move about, talk, laugh and comment upon. Under such an atmosphere the students work because they want to work and not because the teacher wants them to work.

Opportunities to handle and manipulate: Many visual aids offer opportunities to students to handle and manipulate things.

Retentivity: Audio-visual aids contribute to increased retentivity as they stimulate response of the whole organism to the situation in which learning takes place.

Based on maxims of teaching: The use of audio-visual aids enables the teacher to follow the maxims of teaching like 'concrete to abstract', 'known to unknown' and 'learning by doing.'

Helpful in attracting attention: Attention is the true factor in any process of teaching and learning. Audio-visual aids help the teacher in providing proper environment for capturing as well as sustaining the attention and interest of the students in the classroom work.

Helpful in fixing up new learning: 'What is gained in terms of learning, needs to be fixed up in the minds of students. Audiovisual aids help in achieving this objective by providing several activities, experiences and stimuli to the learners'.

Saving of energy and time: A good deal of energy and time of both the teachers and students can be saved on account of the use of audio-visual aids as most of the concepts and phenomena may be easily clarified, understood and assimilated through their use.

Realism: The use of audio-visual aids provides a touch of reality to the learning situation. By seeing a film show exhibiting the life of the people of the Tundra region, students learn it more effectively in about 2 hours than by spending weeks by reading.

Vividness: Audio-visual aids give vividness to the learning situation. A film on Buddha provides a vivid picture of his life and teachings.

Meeting individual differences: There are wide individual differences among learners. Some are ear-oriented, some can be helped through visual demonstrations, while others learn better by doing. The use of a variety of audio-visual aids helps in meeting the needs of different types of students.

Encouragement to healthy classroom interaction: Audio-visual aids, through their wide variety of stimuli, provision of active participation of the students, and vicarious experiences encourage healthy classroom interaction for the effective realization of teaching-learning objectives.

Spread of education on a mass scale: Audio-visaul aids like radio and television help in providing opportunities for education to people living in remote areas. They also help in promoting adult education.

Promotion of scientific temper: In place of listening to facts, students observe demonstrations and phenomena and thus cultivate scientific temper.

Development of higher faculties: Verbalism promotes memorisation. Use of audio-visual aids stirs the imagination, thinking process and reasoning power of the students, and calls for creativity, and inventiveness and other higher mental activities on the parts of students and thus helps the development of higher faculties among the students.

Reinforcement to learners: Audio-visual aids prove effective reinforcers by increasing the probability of re-occurance of the response associated with them and thus render valuable help in the teaching-learning process.

Positive transfer of learning and training: Use of audio-visual aids helps in the learning of other concepts, principles and solving the real problems of life by making possible the appropriate positive transfer of learning and training received in the classroom.

Positive environment for creative discipline: A balanced, rational and scientific use of audio-visual aids develops motivation, attracts the attention and interests of the students and provides a variety of creative outlets for the utilisation of their tremendous energy and thus keeps them busy in the classroom work. In this way, the overall classroom environment becomes conducive to creative discipline.

Six

SPECIAL DIFFICULTIES IN ENGLISH TEACHING

In the school curriculum English as a subject is given great prominence by the authorities. Its study is compulsory for every one. Naturally there are good many teachers of this subject in the schools. But it is rather sad to me that there is something wrong with the teaching of English in Indian schools. *Prof V.K. Gokak* says, "The study of English in our schools is in a chaotic state today- Pupils are taught English for about six periods a week for six years. But it has been estimated that they hardly know 1500 words by the time they join a university. This means that they have hardly been able to learn English words at the rate of one word per period. They do not know how to use the commonest structures of English".

SIGNIFICANCE OF MOTHER TONGUE

Learning of mother tongue takes place in a very natural way. From the birth of a child it is surrounded by an atmosphere where mother tongue is spoken Thus listening by the child goes on and after a few months some meaningful cries are uttered by it. If any error is committed by the child in speaking it is constantly corrected because there are many teachers who are helping it. For learning mother tongue, there is unlimited time and equipment. And above all, everything is learnt quite unconsciously, without straining the mind. In every case, listening and speaking are learnt at home and then the child is sent to school for learning, reading and writing of the language.

A FOREIGN LANGUAGE

The process of learning a foreign language is the same because listening and speaking precede reading and writing. In each case, language is a habit to be got at, activity to be developed, a skill to be practised and enthusiasm to be caught.

Learning a foreign language is an artificial process. The atmosphere of listening or speaking is created for some time but that is not as natural as we have in the case of mother tongue. According to *David Abercrombie*, " The infant has little else to do, has the strongest social compulsion to learn, is continually surrounded by the language it is learning, and has no old habits likely to interfere with what it is doing. But the foreign language learner, whether school-child or adult, is at a disadvantage compared with the infant in so far as he has many other things to do, has sometimes little urge to loam, encounters the language he is learning only at intervals, and finds the native language habits in continual conflict with those needed for the new language. But he is also at an advantage compared with the infant in so far as he possesses a developed intelligence, and is also literate."

When the child learns mother tongue, his mind is a clean slate but at the time of his learning a foreign language, he has already learn his mother tongue. *Robert Paul* says, "When we learn our first language, face the universe directly and loam to clothe it with speech; when we learn a second language, we tend to filter the universe through the language already known. Thus the knowledge of mother tongue helps and it also interferes in the learning of a foreign language. *Prof. Frisby* is of the opinion that, "The process of learning of all languages is almost alike." Thus the skill acquired in the learning of mother tongue helps in acquiring the skill of a foreign language.

INPUT AND OUTPUT SYSTEM

Learning a language is a habit to be got at, an activity to be developed, a skill to be practised and enthusiasm to be caught. It holds true in the learning of any language whether mother tongue or second language or some foreign language, may be English or any other. Another thing needs to be classified here. When mother tongue is learnt the whole process is very natural. While learning English, the process remains artificial whatever may be medium of the school-English or mother tongue. In case of English, the atmosphere of listening or speaking is created for sometime but that is not as natural as we have in the case of mother tongue.

Prof. Frisby put forth the opinion that "The process of learning of all the languages is almost alike. Thus the skill acquired in the learning of mother tongue helps in acquiring the skill of a foreign language. *Ryburn* says, "Any emphasis laid on the mother tongue will have a good effect on the standard of English." *P Gurrey* is of the view, "The teaching of mother tongue and the teaching of a foreign language can support and assist each other."

Interference of Mother Tongue in Learning English:

a. Since no two languages are alike, it is rather difficult to find but exact equivalents of English language in Hindi or Punjabi. If a learner is doing some translation work, it will always be approximate.

b. The alphabets of English are 26 as compared to the alphabets of Punjabi and Hindi which are respectively

35 and 33. These alphabets are used to produce all the sounds. It confuses the mind of the learner.

c. Punjabi and Hindi are phonetic languages- that is their spoken system and writing system are the same. But English is not a phonetic language. So the learner of English faces a number of problem while reading or writing it.

d. A few, consonant sounds of English are not found in Punjabi or Hindi e.g. the initial sound in the words think-, then; the sound occurring in the middle of the words, measure, treasure. Thus the sound of this type create problems for the learner.

e. Stress, intonation and rhythm of the two languages differ widely. That also creates problems for the young learners of English.

f. The sentence patterns of English and mother tongue (Punjabi or Hindi) are quite different. In Punjabi and Hindi, we use Subject, Object and Verb pattern but in English it is 'subject+verb+object.'

   For example:

   It is a table.

g. Interrogative sentences of the two languages are different. In English, the interrogative sentences start with a question word, but in Punjabi or Hindi, such a sentence starts in a simple way.

h. In Punjabi or Hindi, an adjective undergoes a change according to the number or gender, in English it does not change.

   For example:

   Good brother.

   Good brothers.

   Good sister.

i. In Punjabi or Hindi, the verb undergoes a change

according to the gender, but in English it does not change.

For example:

The boy sings.

The girl sings.

j. The structural words of English and Punjabi/Hindi are no equivalent.

For example:

She is a good girl.

The girl is sitting in the chair.

k. In mother tongue, the students form a habit of producing some sounds. For example, they produce sound in some way. While learning English, they come across two sounds. V, W which are different but the learners produce those sounds like mother tongue sounds.

Thus we find that the knowledge of mother tongue helps in learning the language. In many ways, it hinders the effective learning of English. The language teacher should make efforts to overcome the problems in an interesting way.

The poor standards of teaching English in the schools is a problem which needs proper solution. It is high time now that some ways out to tackle this issue be thrashed out. A few suggestions in this regard are given below:

- The teacher should understand fully the different aims of teaching English. He should teach the language keeping the fundamental aims in view. All the aims i.e. listening, speaking, reading and writing are important. He should lay due emphasis on each and teach the learners really. The learners should be enabled to use the language in their day to day life situations.
- The teachers of English should be given training for

the improvement of their own English. Some refresher courses should be organised for them. Attendance in those refresher course should be made compulsory for the teachers. For new recruitment of teachers posts of English teachers should be separated from teachers of social studies. Those who are good in English and have also studied teaching of English at B.Ed. level should be selected. The teachers who have passed some courses in teaching of English from R-I.E. or CIEFL should be given preference in selection. All this will improve the situations.

- It is undoubtedly right that the teachers in the schools use faulty methods of teaching English. Through orientation programmes, they can be acquainted with the latest techniques of teaching English. They will also come to know the effectiveness of various methods in teaching English. Moreover, the teachers-may be asked to attend special training courses in pronunciation.
- The examination system should be improved keeping in view the aims of teaching English in India. Examination should discourage cramming. There should be examinations for testing the different abilities such as listening, speaking, reading and writing. Then there will be real teaching and learning of the language.
- No doubt, India is a poor country and we shall have to adjust more students in the classes. But effort should be made to decrease the number of students. For grammar and composition work, groups comprising lesser number of students may be formed. That will make correction work easier on the part of the teachers. For textbook book teaching, the classes may have more students.
- The physical conditions in the schools should be given special attention by the school authorities. Every school is inspected periodically by the Govt. agencies and by

the supervisors. The authorities concerned should check up the deteriorating situations and make special efforts for improvement. Improvement can be possible provided right type of efforts are made for it.

- The different types of audio-visual aids should be made available in the schools. No doubt, some grants for this purpose have been sanctioned to the schools but more in this direction is needed. The school teachers should also be given training for the handling of different type of sophisticated aids. The teachers should also be acquainted with the libraries from where tapes can be borrowed by the institution for the teaching purpose.
- Textbooks which are prescribed in the schools these days have been nationalised. They have been written by CIFEL and NCERT experts. Even then, some drawbacks in the books continue to be there. The good teachers of the subject and the research workers, should be associated with the task of writing. That will improve things further.
- The curriculum of the school should be carefully planned. It should be made less burdensome and more useful for the learners. It should help the learners to learn things really. The textbooks and other activities in the school fulfil the need and requirements of the children- The curriculum should be practical type.
- Correction work should be understood in its right perspectives by the school authorities. Keeping the total correction work to be done by the teacher in view, load of work should be decided. It will certainly improve the whole situation and help the teacher to teach better and in an effective way.
- As far as possible, the teachers should be encouraged to carry on research in their day to day working in the schools, Research mindedness on the part of the teachers will certainly improve things.

On the basis of suggestions given above, the critical situations in the teaching of English be checked from further deteriorations.

Who is to take the initiative in this direction? Decidedly one or two persons can't do anything solid. Let everyone concerned with it shoulder the responsibility and help bringing a better environment. Only then we could be able to achieve appreciable results in the teaching of English.

COMPLICATIONS AHEAD

Will it be right to say that there is something wrong with the teaching of English? No. The reason is that there is also something wrong with the learning of English in Indian schools. In this context, *Michael West* said "A language is not a subject which can be taught; it is a subject, which must be learnt. " We should make efforts to check the defects. In the words of *Harold Palmer*, "What has been badly assimilated must be eliminated consciously".

If we mirror the whole situation, we are rather astonished to see the sorry state of affairs. Everybody these days is after the examinations. A student does not bother about knowledge or learning of the language. He makes all efforts to get the diploma or degree, no matter what way he is able to get it. For that he follows short-cuts to knowledge. He does not want learning rather he wants prize, money, status etc.

On the other hand, the teacher is after enabling the students to pass the examination. He is always careful that his pass percentage may not go down. Thus there is no real teaching by the teachers or learning by the students in the schools.

The standards of English are fast deteriorating: What makes us feel like that? If we compare the graduate of today with the graduate of a few years back, we notice the marked difference. That graduate was much better. Shall we say that there is something wrong with the learning of English? The fact is that the standards are rather disappearing. The conditions under which English is being taught in the schools are far from satisfactory.

COMPLICATIONS IN THE SYSTEM

The methods of teaching English adopted in the schools are quite defective. The translation method of teaching is used almost in all the schools. The teachers do not show any interest in acquiring knowledge about the lates methods of teaching the subject. They simply enable the students to pass the examination.

For this purpose, they use any cheap method. Even all the aspects of learning a language are ignored. The teacher feels that his job is finished as soon as he has translated something of English into mother tongue. Then they encourage the students for cramming the material. In short, the composition is dictated by the teacher, the textbooks translated into mother tongue and the entire emphasis is on passing the examination through that magic wand of cramming."

PROCEDURE OF ASSESSMENT

The students as well as the teachers have become examination minded. They do every thing just for the sake of examination. The paper setter, the examiner, the teacher etc. don't bother about real teaching-learning of language. The paper setter sets the question paper and only tests the crammed knowledge of the learner The teacher and the students do their work keeping the examination system in view.

Things important from examination point of view are taken up. There is no examination for spoken English. So every body ignores this important aspect of learning the language. The fear of the examination remains taxing for the teachers and the students. There is hardly any learning in the real sense of the word.

FUNCTIONS OF THE GUARDIAN

Interference by the parents in the work of the teachers hinders the progress. When the teacher makes efforts to apply the new ways of teaching English, he faces a set back due to the interference of the parents whose children are studying there. The parents may be of orthodox type. They themselves were taught in same way.

If the teacher spends time on giving the learners just listening and speaking practice, the parents feel as if nothing has been taught. They judge the work on the basis of written exercises only. Under such circumstances the teacher has to change himself, his methodology and teach the way the parents like. Thus undue interference of the parents deteriorates the situations.

ACHIEVEMENTS

The teachers in the schools teach English and the learners learn English but none of them is fully clear about the real purpose of teaching-learning English. The different items of the syllabus are covered in the class. Every time the teachers as well as the learners consider it as a knowledge subject and not as a skill subject. They are not clear about the aims of teaching English. The teacher is like a sailor who does not know his destination and the pupil is like a rudderless vessel which may be drifted along anywhere ashore.

ABILITY OF A TEACHER

Many teachers of English who are teaching the subject are not competent. Very few of them are really competent for teaching this subject. They have defective pronunciation. They have hardly a satisfactory command over English. At the time of selection thy are taken up as Social Studies master and mistresses and not as English masters or mistresses. Moreover, in the selection, no body gives any weightage to the subject.

Teaching of English, studied at B. Ed. level. They are selected on the basis of their subjects studied upto B.A. level.

In this context, the *English Review Committee* appointed by U.G.C. in 1965 said, "There is a shortage of teachers. Those available have just passed the school final examination, having themselves studied English in a village school for 4 or 5 or 6 years. They have little idea of correct usage, and not at all of correct pronunciation. Their vocabulary is limited as is their reading."

With the lapse of some more time, we find that now better qualified teachers are available. But in basic qualifications, they are lacking all the more. Their knowledge of English is inadequate. *Prof V.K Gokak* in his book, 'English in India, its Present and Future' has rightly said, "The foundational years for the teaching of English in school are in the hands of teachers who neither know enough English nor are familiar with the latest and far reaching developments in the pedagogy of English".

RESEARCH NECESSITY

Teaching-learning process needs continuous overhauling. The drawbacks in the teaching-learning of English may be many, but their solutions need be thought of. Who should do this? The teachers of English, the research minded scholars can do it. A good teacher does not teach the same thing in the same way year after year. He is always on the look out for introducing new things in new ways. In this fast changing age of science and technology, research on the part of the teachers is very essential. But we find that the teachers are not able to carry on any research. The lack of research deteriorates the situations.

Thus we find that the conditions under which English is being taught in the schools are not satisfactory. The different factors be checked properly. All efforts should be made to remedy the draw-backs.

Only then the deteriorating situations will improve. *Ronald Mackin* has summed up the defects. "The old-fashioned type of benches and desks which restrict movement, the bad light; the noise from neighbouring classes which may he separated from them by nothing more than a bamboo screen; insufficient provision for their subject in the time-table, lack of aids of all kinds interference from parents or a dominating, conservative Headmaster; and finally the requirements of an examination system which places a premium on the written language and consequently seems to favour the grammar-grinder of the old school".

Seven

PLACE OF ENGLISH IN EDUCATION

The language is a means through which a child contemplates the past, grasps the present and approaches the future. It goes without saying that the language plays an important role in the mental, emotional and social development of a person. Though English is a foreign language yet it occupies a unique position in our country.

Whether we are at home, in the state or out of it, in the country or away from it, English is important and it continues to hold a unique position. How much is that importance? It is a very pertinent question. In order to understand it fully, we shall have to study the history of this language in our country.

Undoubtedly, Hindi is one of the most important languages of the country. But as a link language, Hindi has not been accepted on the whole by people in the South. Hence English has been given the status of the Associate Official Language of the country.

Professor P. Gurrey writes in his book "Teaching English as a Foreign Language'- "All languages are used for the same purpose ....they are used, for insurance, for communication, for expressing anything that we have attended to, for recording information, for thinking, for getting what we want, and so on." Whatever may be the language, say English, Hindi, Punjabi, Chinese, Russian, French, Germany or any other, the purpose of each is the same i.e. communication, expressing, recording, thinking etc.

In our country, English was introduced about two centuries ago. It is rather interesting to know how this language gradually got prominence. In the Charter of 1813, article 433 was a pious clause which changed the whole lot of the people. The said clause authorised the Governor-General in Council to spend a sum of not less that one lac of rupees in each year on the revival and improvement of literature ....for the introduction and promotion of a knowledge of the science.... among the British territories in India. With this, a background for British education was prepared.

Later with the coming of Lord Macaulay, the man behind modern education in India, it was clarified how the sum of one lac of rupees was to be spent. That was the time when the foreign plant of English' was sown in Indian soil. Lord Macaulay clarified the meanings of the words like literature, medium of instruction, agency of education etc. Thereafter the study of English was made compulsory. Soon English became the medium of instruction. The supremacy of English led to many controversies. After 1857, the common feeling was to oust the Britishers from the Indian soil.

On seeing the plight of Indian students, Gandhiji wrote, "our boys think that without English they cannot get Government service. Girls are taught English as passport for marriage. The canker has so eaten into the society that in many cases the only meaning of education is a knowledge of English.

All these are for me signs of our slavery and degradation." He condemned the study of English at the cost of the study of mother tongue. M.K. Gandhi further said, " I would have our young men and women with literary tastes to learn as much of English and other world languages as they like...... But I would not have a single Indian to forget, neglect or be ashamed of his mother tongue ....

ELITE LANGUAGE

Whatever has been said in *Kothari Education Commission Report* regarding the place of English is perfectly true because they have taken into consideration its present position in the country. The point is that at present everybody is talking against this language. The conditions prevailing in the schools are not favourable. The politicians, the parents and the public in general are saying rot about this language. Their inner desire is to uproot this language from the country. Many teachers are seen finding faults with the students.

Sometimes they say that it is next to impossible to show good results in English. The authorities have also expressed the view that it would be difficult to progress without the knowledge of English. So Kothari Education Commission has suggested that English should be made a library language in our country That way our scholars who are doing advanced studies in the field of Science, Medicine, Engineering etc. will be able to consult library books. Advanced knowledge and excellent literature of the world be in the books which are in English medium.

Indian readers must have at least as much knowledge of English as is required to understand the books lying in the library. Without the study of English books, there can be every possibility of duplication in labour. Only the study of English books reveals the degree of advancement that has taken place so far in the world. Our scholars by the study of those books, can acquaint themselves fully with the subject matter and they may think of going ahead in that direction or a new era of researches may be found out by them.

Thus Kothari Education Commission has said that it is rather advisable to make it a library language. In fact, making English a library language in the country will be nothing short of accepting defeat in the teaching-learning of this language.

By library language, we mean that the carriers must study that much English which should help them to understand the subject matter contained in library books. They may not become fluent speakers of the language. They may not even acquire the ability of writing nicely in correct English. But they must learn English which should ensure them comprehension of the reading material. So the ultimate aim here is to teach reading.

Now the question arises whether reading cart be taught without giving practice. No, it is not possible. For all purposes, we must begin with speech. Practice in listening is needed -which will help in speaking. Speech is important for learning reading of the language. The ability to recognise the written symbols comes through continuous practice and for reading out those very symbols, speech is required. So by starting with speech, language should be learnt and the ultimate aim should be reading with comprehension. Only then a person will be able to use English as a library language.

English is, therefore, an important language and it must be studied. *Prof Gokak* has rightly observed that "it was in the English classroom that the Indian library renaissance was born." A few words from *Kothari Education Commission Report* are worth quoting," English as an important library language would play vital role in higher education. No student should be considered as qualified for a degree, in particular, a Master's degree unless he has acquired a reasonable proficiency in English."

So it is a decided fact that English is an important library language. If some people say that it is a difficult language and hence cannot be taught well in our country, it is their weakness. As a teacher of English I am of the opinion that English can be taught and it should be taught as a living language in the country. If all teachers of English determine and fight against the bad situations, there is no reason why they will not be able to succeed in this direction. The newly evolved approaches may be made use of and by applying sincere and honest efforts, the English language can be taught as it should be taught for its success and bright future in the country.

IMPORTANCE OF ENGLISH

"We in our anger and the hatred against the British people should not throw away the baby (English) with the bath water (English people)".

In the history of English in India, we find that English has dominated the teaching learning programme from the beginning. Never was there any hatred or grudge against this language. It has been taught and learnt with affection and love. It has definitely enjoyed a privileged position. The persons not studying it might have felt some sort of inferiority complex. There have been good teachers of this subject not only foreigners alone but Indians as well. Some of them came out to be more sincere and dedicated to the teaching of this language. With them, a study of the subject was always a point of inspiration. They have not only done their duties but in addition they have also contributed a lot.

It goes without saying that English is a language borrowed from six thousand miles away and it belongs to an entirely different nation. But that does not mean that it has no relationship with us. Every human being is free to study any language. English is not only a national language of the English men, it is an international language. It may be called the language of the world civilization. Its richness, its flexibility, its elegance, its dignity seem to have made it universally popular. Even M.K. Gandhi said' in 'Thoughts of National Languages' "I hold its knowledge as a second language to be indispensable for specified Indians who have to represent the country's interest in the international domain. I regard the English language as an open window for peeping into western thought and science'. In other words, Gandhiji accepted the importance of this language for the selected few people who are to hold the reigns of the motherland. In this age of democracy, every one can dream of holding the charge of the country. Naturally none can be denied the study of this language. Pt. Nehru said, 'English language is our's by-historic necessity."

The different points explained here below show very clearly that English has its unique importance in our country. We can hardly bear dispensing with it from our mother land.

A Link Language: In our country, we have different states with different regional languages. People living in these states use their own languages for conversation, discussion etc. But English is a language which links them together. The leaders from different states meet sometimes formally over a common platform.

By using this language, they can convey to one another their heart felt desires and thus they can share the views of one another. In the words of Pt. Nehru, "The language link is a greater link between us and English speaking people than any political link or common wealth link or anything else. It is so because we can see how their thoughts are functioning, much more than in other European languages." Thus, we find that the use of English in our country has been a unifying factor.

Pt. Nehru once said, "If you push out English, does Hindi fully take its place? I hope it will. I am sure it will. But I wish to avoid the danger of one unifying factor being pushed out without another unifying factor fully taking its place. In that event, there will be a gap. The creation of any such gap must be avoided at all costs. It is this that leads me to the conclusion that English is likely to have an important place in the foreseeable future." Besides, we can keep our links with the outside world by using English language.

Prof. R.S. Trivedi points out, "India's connection with the Common Wealth, the U.N.O. and its agencies, her needs of foreign trade and economic aid from different countries, her need for the technical know-how for her development and her role in the affairs of the world, all conjointly enjoin upon the framers of her educational policy to give due weight to English so that her interests do not suffer and she does not detract from her rightful place in the world policy."

Educational Importance: From educational point of view, English played a prominent role in the past. Before independence, it was the medium of instruction both at the school stage and the college stage. Higher education in Science, medicine, engineering, technology etc. was not possible without English. Even now advanced studies in these areas are not possible without the knowledge of English. Good books in all these subjects are available in English only. But Indian languages have not been developed enough to meet the demands of the difficult subjects. If we decide to give up English altogether, we would cut ourselves off from the living stream of ever growing knowledge.

Role in Trade, Industry and Commerce: English plays an important role in the industrial and commercial life of the country. All correspondence is done mainly in English. National and international trade, development of industry and the working in commercial establishments take place in English. Efficiency and success in these fields depends upon an adequate knowledge of English. Their maintenance of accounts, issuing of instructions and correspondence with others are mainly conducted through English medium.

International Status: As English is spoken and understood all over the globe, so it has got international importance. It is the first language in U.K., U.S.A., Canada and Australia and the second language in India, Africa, Russia, France, Pakistan etc. The number of people speaking this language is about 350 million which is next to the Chinese language. Thus it is English and other language which can serve the purpose of linking together people of different nations of the world.

Chinese language is confined to that country only whereas English is popular with people living in different countries of the world. Naturally its popularity on the basis of its utility all over the globe determines its strength. It is English language which can bring greater and greater number of people in closer contacts with one another. It helps every nation to study the culture and civilization of the other nation. It is through English that we can establish political, cultural, intellectual and economic relations with the rest of the world.

F.G. French in his book, 'Teaching English as an International Language' says:

> "By accidents of history and by the rapid spread of industrial development, science and technology, international trade, and by something like an explosion in the speed and ease of travel and by all factors which have broken down frontiers and forced nations into closer interdependence, English has become a world language. It is the means of international communication : there is no other."

So English language is indispensable for us. Even Mahatma Gandhi had to say, "English is a language of international commerce; it is the language of diplomacy and it contains many a rich literary treasure; it gives us an introduction to western thought and culture."

The following points indicate very clearly the international importance of English language:

(i) It helps in international trade and industry.

(ii) It leads to better understanding between the different nations of the world.

(iii) The latest and up-to-date information in the field of science and technology is available in English only.

(iv) A person knowing English stands opportunities of employment almost in every country.

(v) It helps in bringing people of different nations in closer contacts.

Cultural Values: English helps in bringing people of diverse cultures closer to each other. It also assists us for our inter-cultural understanding inside the country. It is through the medium of English that we are able to keep the different cultural groups of India united. In fact, English has helped us in building new cultural traditions. It has also resulted in the process of modernisation of Indian society.

The study of English culture has dispelled ignorance and superstitions from the minds of the Indian people. English language has imported the wealth of the Indian people. English language has imported the wealth of knowledge and experiences in India. To abolish it will be to shut the doors of the western culture and civilization for Indian students. Thus from the cultural point of view English has great importance. It has become the next powerful vehicle of our thought and activity. It is, undoubtedly, a language of modern scientific culture.

Window on the World: The study of English by Indians serves the purpose of a window. Just as we can peep through the window and see what is happening all around us. In the same way, by the study of English we can come to know the progress being made by the people of different nations oil the world in the different areas of life. F.G. French rightly observed. "A traveller who can speak English will find some body who can understand him wherever he may go: anyone who can read English can keep in touch with the whole world without leaving his own house."

In fact, in Pt. Nehru's words "Our major window on the modern world" regarding English language are quite apt. Radhakrishnan's University Education Commission remarked, "It (English) is a language which is rich in literature-humanistic, scientific and technical. If under sentimental urges we give up English, we would cut ourselves off from the living stream of evergrowing knowledge. Unable to have access to this knowledge, our standards of scholarship would fast deteriorate and our participation in the world movements of thought would become negligible. Its effects would be disastrous for our political life, for living nations must move with the items and must respond quickly to the challenges to their surroundings. English is the only means of preventing our isolation from the world and will act unwisely if we allow ourselves to be enveloped in the fold of a dark curtain of ignorance. Our students who are undergoing training at schools, which will admit them, either to university or to vocation must acquire sufficient mastery of English to give them access to the treasures of knowledge and in the universities no student should be allowed to take a degree who does not acquire the ability to read with facility and understanding works of English authors."

Thus we find that English informs us about the advancement or progress having taken place or taking place throughout the world. It may be the field of science, technology, machine or it may be any human activity we come to know about it through this language. It is a highly developed language and it mirrors to us everything in the true sense. Our country cannot afford to close the window because it gives us true picture of the various facets of life-political social, religious, cultural, agricultural etc. Here the words of Mr. Nehru, our late Prime Minister are worth quoting. He said, "All regional languages must be developed and promoted. But that did not mean that English should be discarded. To do that will amount to closing a window on the world of technology. Foreign languages served as window in the world of technology. Foreign languages served as window on it and to suppose that translation could take their place was a mistake. It was no use getting into an intellectual prison after achieving political independence.

Role in our Social Life: English is playing an equally important role in the social life of Indian People. Majority of educated people use this language for correspondence. They find it more convenient to converse in English. It is the means of social and intellectual communication in the highly educated sections of society. In marriage parties or at the time of some social ceremony, the invitation cards are mostly printed in English. In our daily conversation we use a large number of English words. It has become such a habit with us that in our speech we use English words and find dearth of words of our own languages.

English at the Administrative Level: English has been the official language in our country, for more than 150 years. Even now, this language has almost the same position in the offices of the country. No doubt, some states have made strong efforts for developing their own regional languages and propagated its use in the offices. But the hard fact is that in majority cases, they have not been able to replace English. Almost at every level of administration we find that English alone is being used. In the District courts, High Courts and the Supreme Court, cases are presented in English. So it remains a proved fact that English dominates in our country at the different levels of administration.

Already Known to Indians: In this age of competitions, every one wants to excel the other. Some people are interested in learning more languages. The need to learn some foreign language is there. Now the question arises which foreign language should be learnt.

English is a language already prevalent in our country since long. We have people who can teach this language and also we have English literature produced by our own country men. So instead of thinking about some other language, it would be better if we learn this very language, We have a suitable climate for it already created in our country. Regarding English language Pt. Nehru once said, "We know it a good deal and we have people who can teach it."

Knowledge of English a Successful Passport for Employment: The knowledge of English provides a privileged position to a person. People with good knowledge of English are given preference for selection to good posts. The prospects of employment for a person knowing English are bright anywhere whether India or abroad. S.K. Chatterji rightly says. It (English) is, therefore, pre-eminently the language which opens to us prospects of employment at home and abroad and offers means of cultural communication with other parts of the world. Knowledge of English is an asset with any person post.

A person with knowledge of English stands good chances of employment anywhere and everywhere in the world. F.G. French rightly says in this connection- "English is rapidly becoming a world language. It is the mother tongue of more than two hundred million people; and, in addition, it is spoken and read by many millions of Europeans, Africans, Chinese, Indians, Japanese and South Americans as a second language."

The Radhakrishnan Commission emphasized; English is the means of preventing our isolation from the world and we will act unwisely if we allow ourselves to be enveloped in the folds of a dark curtain of ignorance. A sense of oneness of the world is in the making and control over a medium of expression which is more widespread and has a large reach than any of our languages today will be of immense benefit to us."

Thus we find that English plays quite an important role in our national life. Almost from every angle, it is significant for us. In the past, it enjoyed a privileged position in our country. Now also its position is in no way less as compared to other languages. Inspite of the bare fact that mother tongue as medium of instruction almost at all levels of learning has been accepted at Govt. level but the hard fact means that more and more English medium schools are coming up and greater and greater number of people are becoming interested in those English medium schools. All this speaks clearly about the dominating position of English language in our country On this basis, we can calculatively fore see that the future of English in our country will be as bright as ever.

ROLE OF BRITISHERS

During the pre-independence period, English enjoyed the privileged position. During that time it was:

Queen of Languages: During the British rule over India, English enjoyed the topmost position. It was the first language in the whole country. It was the *lingua franca* of the literate. It was considered to be the queen of the languages. In every walk of life, it was the vehicle of thought and activity. The importance given to it was the envy of every one and in no way it created any jealousy. It was the pride of all.

Medium of Instruction at Different Levels: English used to be the medium of instruction at school and college levels. In some of the elementary schools also, English was used as a medium of instruction. Every body loved to study different subjects through this language.

Englishmen Teaching English: The study of English was meant for all the children who joined the school. Our elders speak English very nicely. The main reason behind is that they were taught mostly by the English men. All subjects whether English, History or Geography were generally taught by the English men. Thus the students were under the impact of the English men for a good deal of time. They listened to spoken English of the native speakers. That is why our elderly persons whose schooling careers belong to that era, can speak 'A Class English.'

INITIAL PHASE

The study of English was introduced on the day the child entered the school. Every body was proud of it because the study of this language was considered a passport for employment. Thus we find that English was of great importance before the freedom of our country. But with the passage of time, there have come about a number of changes in the position of English in our country.

In 1947, India became free and the English people left India for good. The whole administration, the language policy etc. came into the hands of Indian authorities. The very question regarding the place of English in India became controversial. Some leaders argued that English should be uprooted from the country, whereas some others favoured the retention of English. Mahatma Gandhi said, "It is my considered opinion that English education, in the manner it has been given, has emasculated the English educated Indians. It has put a severe strain upon the Indian students and made us imitators."

He further said, "all the superstitions that India has, none is so great as that, a knowledge of the English language is necessary for imbibing ideas of liberty and developing accuracy of thought." But other persons like C. Rajgopalachary say that English should be retired in the country. Their considered opinion was-" We in our anger and the hatred against the British people should not throw away the baby (English) with the bath water (English people)."

Maulana Abul Kalam Azad, soon after taking over the education portfolio in the Interim Government, said at a press conference: "So far as general studies are concerned it was never my intention to suggest that there should be any fall in the standard of English." In the words of Pt. Nehru "One hundred and fifty years of intimate contact has made English an integral part of our educational system and this cannot be changed without injury to the cause of education in India. In addition English has today become one of the major languages of the world and Indians can neglect its study only at the risk of loss of themselves. I am convinced that in the future as well, the standard of teaching English should be maintained at as high a level as possible."

In fact, for the first two or three years of independence, so much was said but nothing concrete could be decided. In 1950, when Indian Constitution was framed, it was unanimously decided to continue English as the official language of the country for fifteen years. During this period all efforts were made to develop Hindi-the national language of the country. The Indian authorities, thus, hoped to replace English by Hindi in due course of time. But there was great opposition by the people living in southern part of the country. The result was that in 1963, the Parliament passed a bill according to which English was declared to be the Associate Official Language of India for an indefinite period. In 1968, the National Policy on Education adopted by the Govt. of India stressed, "Special emphasis needs to be laid on the study of English and other international languages. World knowledge is growing at a tremendous pace, especially in science and technology. India must not only keep up this growth, but also make her own significant contribution to it. For this purpose, study of English deserves to be specially strengthened." With the passage of time, some of the states adopted their regional language as the official language. But they could not make Hindi as the link language between the different states. The reason is that Hindi is not understood in the different states of free India. So in order to continue links between various states of India, English continues to be the unifying factor.

Reddy T. Prabhaker writes in the Journal of English Language Teaching (1977), 'The number of Indian writers who use English for creative writing is increasing gradually. It looks as if it has become one of the languages of India and its long and wide use by the Indian intelligentia has given it a distinct identity.'

COMPLICATIONS IN LANGUAGE LEARNING

Language is a means of communication without which the society is not able to make progress. In some countries, there is no language problem. In India, the language problem exists because there are many languages used in different states of the country. Due to different social groups in our country, the language problem has been there due to one reason or the other. Every body loves mother tongue and every body likes his regional language.

Then interest of the national language i.e. Hindi cannot be sacrificed. There are some parts of India where people are not ready to accept Hindi. Therefore, the language problem in our country has to be cared for and proper solution has to be thought of.

Before independence and immediately after independence, the medium of instruction in secondary and higher education was English. Gradually shift in the medium of instructions at all levels was made from English to mother tongue or the regional language of the area. Officially all that was done and the problem with regard to the medium of instruction was solved at Government level. But the hard fact is that during the last two decades, a large number of English medium schools have cropped up. Keeping the ever growing demand of the people for English medium schools, more and more English medium schools are being established not only in cities but also in rural areas. Its effect on Government schools have also been felt by all concerned. Recently some state Governments have announced the introduction of English from first standard. Some other state Governments are considering the issue of introducing English from first standard. Rather it has become a serious problem with them. Discussions and debates are going on there.

THREE-LANGUAGE SCHEME

Different committees and commissions have given their suggestions to solve the language problem in the country. The Central Advisory Board of Education (1956) designed a three language formula and recommended it for the school children. Then in 1961, the Chief Ministers' Conference endorsed the three language formula for the schools. According to the three language formula, every school going child was required to study the following three languages.

(i) Mother tongue or the regional language

(ii) English

(iii) Hindi for non-Hindi speaking areas

(iv) If mother tongue is Hindi, then another modern Indian language. Thus if mother tongue of the child is Urdu, he/ she will have to study Urdu, English and Hindi. On the other hand, if the mother tongue of the child is Hindi, he will be required to learn, Hindi, English and one more Indian language. Thus in Punjab, the students learn Punjabi, English and Hindi and in Haryana, the students learn Hindi, English and Punjabi. In U.P., the students learn Hindi, English and Sanskrit.

Kothari Education Commission (1964-66) modified the dum language formula. According to the commission, regional language should be taught at the lower primary stage (class I to class IV). At the higher primary stage (class v to class vi) mother tongue or Hindi/mother tongue or English should be taught compulsorily and the third language should be taught on optional basis. In classes VII to X, the students should study three languages. Thus in Hindi speaking areas, the students will study Hindi, English and a modern Indian language. In non-Hindi speaking areas, the pupils will study regional language, Hindi and English.

Thus we find that English has to be learnt by one and all in the schooling period. Now in this age of science and technology, every one is conscious of making improvements. Without English, it is not possible. Now more and more people are getting ready to learn English.

SCHOOL SYLLABUS

In school curriculum, English occupies an important place. In some states, English is introduced in class I in Govt. schools and Govt. aided schools. Its study is compulsory for all the students. Pass in the examination in this subject is essential. In the case of central schools, English as one subject is introduced in the standard 1. In schools affiliated to C.B.S.E. also, English is introduced in standard 1.

Now when the regional languages are becoming important day by day in every state of the country, the status of English can be considered from the following points of view:

(i) English as an international language.

(ii) English as our major window on the world.

(iii) English as a link language.

(iv) English as a library language.

Eight

SIGNIFICANCE OF TEXTBOOKS

Textbooks are a part of book publishing, which have a significant place in education and publication industry. In many countries, the printing industry lacks modern equipment that can provide short print runs economically. With the exception of the Russian Federation most countries need to import paper.

Printing prices in the Republic of Moldova, which had been a major printing centre in the Soviet Union, are low in comparison with those in neighbouring countries and there is substantial demand for its services from Romania. Bulgaria and the Russian Federation. Many countries must find financing for short-run textbooks to meet minority needs. There is an urgent need for training in writing, publishing and distribution of textbooks, and for training of teachers in their use.

The Open Society Institute and the local Soros Foundations for Open Society have been running numerous regional and general programmes addressing educational reforms, textbook publication and translation of materials. The British Know

How Fund has also organized training workshops in Albania and Romania. In the early 1990s the Soros Foundation supported some 400 writing projects in the Russian Federation, most of them supplementary materials that have found their way to the country's more progressive schools.

The World Bank is supporting the publication and distribution of selected primary and secondary school core textbooks in Bosnia and Herzegovina. In Romania, it supported an education reform project that introduced new textbooks and competition. It is negotiating with Albania an education reform loan that would include competitive textbooks. It has also provided support for textbooks in the Russian Federation, the Former Yugoslav Republic of Macedonia, and the Republic of Moldova. A Bank project in the Russian Federation involved direct loans to oblasts to provide working capital for publishers to produce federally approved textbooks, but it faltered, just as agreement was to be signed, after the ruble was devalued in August 1998.

Strategies for developing, publishing and distributing textbooks and other learning materials must be devised to meet local conditions and needs. They should be based on what is appropriate and practical locally, not on an imported model. None the less, some thirty lessons may be drawn from the achievements and the failures of the decade since Jomtien.

Depending on the quality of their binding and paper, if they are well used and well cared for they may last three years, or even five. Where, children carry them home each day over hilly paths, in seasons of heavy rain, to homes without shelves, they may not last that long. In northwestern Pakistan, the simple saddle-stitched textbooks are not expected to last longer than one year and those for the early grades, whose owners have not yet been trained in book care, often must be replaced part-way through the year.

Textbooks must also survive domestic hazard. Younger

siblings are always a threat and an extremely unlucky student may find his illiterate father has torn a page from a textbook to roll his tobacco in or his mother has taken a page for wrapping the sugar she is selling. In time, moreover, and regardless of their physical condition, textbooks grow obsolete as the curriculum changes and so must be replaced. As a result, textbooks have never fit comfortably into the large-scale projects and procurement procedures of the World Bank and other funding agencies' institutions that were designed initially to help fund long-lasting capital projects such as dams, bridges and roads.

Open competitive bidding that is based principally on cost can be used in procuring the paper and printing for textbooks, but fails when it is applied to textbooks that are individually unique and cannot truly be compared as simple commodities. While the World Bank has never stipulated that it looks for the cheapest price, procurement has been affected by a shortage of qualified staff and a less than perfect implementation of general guidelines for procurement, including a trial set of guidelines for procurement of textbooks issued in 1994.

In countries where state institutions wrote, produced and distributed a single textbook for each subject/level, the systems generally have been found to be inefficient and ineffective. Sida found that in the programmes it supported, by and large government publishing has not functioned well. State-aided companies are frequently hampered by inefficient bureaucracy, unawareness of real costs, or lack of motivation on the part of the staff. Other observers have noted that hidden subsidies masked true costs. Civil servants often well versed in educational theory but unskilled in printing and publishing techniques made decisions that might be pedagogically appropriate but unnecessarily costly. Books were produced in uneconomical page sizes and in wasteful designs.

Distribution systems failed because of inadequate funding

for transportation from regional warehouses to the schools. Everywhere, books were frequently late in reaching the schools, if they arrived at all; too often they remained in regional and district storerooms, ill protected from water, mould, insects and vermin.

Textbook provision suffered from the common maladies of a civil service. Functions were sometimes scattered among different departments or units, with little coordination. Personnel were poorly motivated to meet schedules or save money. Staff development and promotion followed civil service procedures, often oblivious to publishing professionalism: staff were transferred to publishing units on the basis of seniority or availability rather than knowledge or merit.

Rules and procedures for procurement were cumbersome. Funding was principally by an annual legislative grant, making forward planning difficult if not impossible. The contents of textbooks often reflected the values and policies of the government that controlled the purse strings and appointments.

COLLABORATIVE PUBLICATION

For nascent publishing industries, the fastest route to sustainability may be through cooperation. It may be through adaptation of a textbook produced in a neighbouring country, such as the science series developed on a Kenyan model that gave Fountain Publishers of Uganda rapid access to a newly liberalized market. Or it may be a joint venture between a local publishing house and a well-established house in an industrialized country, involving the transfer of know-how as well as capital, as happened in Jamaica, Mali, Cameroon and Namibia.

An impressive example of cooperation between local and non-local companies is the partnership of Heinemann Educational Publishers of the United Kingdom and New Namibia Books. When it began in 1990, the local partner consisted only of its owner, who had recently returned from England with no resources.

By 1997, the collaboration had produced two core textbook courses, in primary and junior secondary school science, for a country that had been almost totally dependent on South African imports. New Namibia Books had eight qualified employees and an extensive list of other books that it had developed with profits from textbooks.

Intergovernmental cooperation is also possible. In examples described above, several countries of French-speaking sub-Saharan Africa established common curricula and developed common textbooks in order to achieve economies of scale. The potential of intergovernmental cooperation was also recognized by a group of English-speaking and Portuguese speaking policy and decision-makers, educational planners, curriculum developers and textbook development managers from ten African countries at a seminar in 1991.

They suggested cooperation was particularly appropriate for countries and island communities whose populations were too small to make the local production of school books, economical or sustainable.

Sub-regional clusters of such countries could form common examination councils and develop standardized curricula, opening possibilities for regional negotiations with publishers for bulk supply and bulk prices. Regional adoptions to achieve economies of scale in procurement were subsequently recommended for the countries of the Organization of Eastern Caribbean States.

Few programmes along these lines have been implemented, however. A common textbook implies a common language of instruction, normally a metropolitan language as in the francophone example, in contrast to a trend towards use of local languages. Brunswic and Hajjar have observed, moreover, that in their experience cooperation is more difficult to develop between governmental institutions than between commercial publishers.

In principle, cooperation between publishers in neighbouring countries should be practicable. Curricula differ across borders, but in many instances are similar enough for transactional companies to adapt the textbook used in one country for adoption in another. Local publishers should be able to do the same. Cooperative ventures are impeded, however, by lack of information, poor communications, ineffective marketing, national bias, customs and tariff barriers, foreign exchange restrictions and cumbersome bureaucracies.

In higher-level subjects such as science and mathematics, imported books will probably continue to play an important role. In primary-level subjects, especially those without a major socio-cultural component, co-publication and adaptations should be expected to increase. Within Africa, the value of trade in books of all kinds between countries doubled between 1992 and 1996, and the Zimbabwe International Book Fair annually reports increasing international business. At this year's fair, just over one-third of exhibitors and visitors responding to a questionnaire said they had come to negotiate, confirm or revisit co-publishing agreements.

Until then, Jordanian statistics had been gathered centrally on an outdated mainframe computer, in flat files not easily amenable to statistical applications, in a form principally dictated by the Educational Statistics Yearbook. The Ministry of Education and twenty-three regional directorates collected their own information and held it in their own locations, usually in manual records. To complicate matters further, the identification number of each school changed every year.

The system could report gross enrolment and student flow rates, but the aggregated data could not be disaggregated for analysis or for comparison, for example, between districts or schools or between schools and an absolute standard. For the new system, personal computers were bought, relational database programmes installed, staff trained at the central and regional levels, and EMIS operations gradually transferred to the regional offices. At the end of five years, data entry time had been reduced from about six months to two weeks and the accuracy of data was substantially improved.

The Jordanian experience demonstrates that, with proper initial technical assistance and guidance, and even modest means, a developing country can improve its educational information-gathering dramatically.

Innovation in curricula is necessary to introduce new learning and new methodology. But abrupt or frequent changes can throw the textbook provision system into disarray and discourage publishers from investing in textbook development. The provincial textbook boards in Pakistan, for example, used to complain about the almost annual small revisions that issued from the federal curriculum developers in Islamabad, forcing minor but expensive changes in the textbooks published provincially.

In the Philippines, a Secretary of Education decided to reinstate science as a subject in the first two primary grades just two years after his predecessor had removed it from the curriculum; science was therefore officially on the curriculum, but there were no textbooks to teach it and relatively few teachers trained to teach it without such help.

Commercial textbook publishers in particular seek stability in curricula. In order to keep the price of textbooks as low as possible, they are anxious to amortize the substantial costs of development (writing, editing, design, illustration, typesetting, and field testing) over three to five years of sales. If the curriculum changes significantly during that period, they cannot recoup their investment. If they have printed books in anticipation of sales under the old curriculum, they will have a warehouse full of unsaleable books. For these reasons, when the Philippines moved from state to commercial production of textbooks in 1995, the publishers requested and were granted a guarantee that no substantial changes would be made in the curriculum for five years.

The impact of abrupt change on commercial publishing may be seen in South Africa, where the government of Nelson Mandela made two major changes in educational structure and policy. The first was to unite the fragmented apartheid system of eighteen education departments into one national department that sets policy and nine provincial departments that are responsible for operations.

The second was to promulgate a new curriculum that is outcomes-based, a radical shift from the authoritarian system that existed under apartheid. The new curriculum was to be introduced at the rate of two grades per year. The schedule was stretched out subsequently, but publishers initially set out to develop, write, design and produce textbooks for Grades I and 7 in just 18 months and to do so in most, if not all, of the eleven official languages. That they achieved as much as they did was remarkable, although most were forced to cut back to three to five languages besides English and Africans.

When the date for implementation in Grade 7 was deferred, publishers were faced with development costs but no sales. There were problems with the selection and authorization of textbooks, in part because of inadequate training of evaluators and in part because of bureaucratic rigidity, and decisions were inconsistent between and within provinces.

Books were often delivered after the beginning of the school year. Budgets for buying books were far less than expected. The government had promised a free and equal education for all children up to Grade 9, with a book on every child's desk; in fact, however, the money for textbook acquisition dropped more than 80 per cent between 1996 and 1998 as the bulk of the educational budget was consumed by increased teachers' salaries, and a promised increase in 1999 fell far below what was required.

The consequences to what had been a well-established and confident publishing industry have been devastating. Companies faced with high overhead costs for the development of new textbooks and severely reduced markets have started retrenching. An estimated 44 per cent of the educational publishing industry has been lost in the last eighteen months a demonstration of the fragility of an industry that depends upon a single customer.

State purchase of textbooks for free distribution through the schools is desirable to ensure equity in education, but few of the countries surveyed have been able to meet a target textbook: pupil ratio of 1:1 or 1:2 throughout their jurisdiction or to sustain that level even with external assistance. To maintain free distribution, the state must commit funds annually to production or purchase, distribution, warehousing and supervision.

Few have been willing to do so in the requisite amounts and budgetary shortfalls usually affect the districts already most disadvantaged. Both Jamaica and Mexico did achieve the target during the early 1990s, but at the cost of inferior books in Jamaica and ballooning cumulative expenditures in Mexico. Furthermore, free distribution discourages private booksellers who are the key to continuing literacy and engenders a belief that books should never be paid for. Even politicians begin to consider books free commodities.

Unless a state has the both the tax base and the political will to allocate sufficient amounts of public money for the provision of learning materials, it will continue to be dependent on external support or have to attempt some form of cost recovery. Both may be necessary.

The state can relieve itself of all or part of the financial burden of textbook provision by expecting families to pay for the textbooks their children use, just as they may be expected to pay for uniforms or work books. This approach penalizes the disadvantaged. Poor families may not be able to afford to buy textbooks and families living in remote areas may have no access to them for lack of retail outlets stocking them.

Families may have to choose which children to educate, usually at the expense of girls. They may also discriminate between subjects, buying textbooks only in those subjects that seem most likely to lead directly to future employment. This system does encourage private bookselling and instils the book buying habit. Governments can subsidize the cost of production to reduce the cost to families, as happened in Cote d'Ivoire after the radical devaluation of the CFA franc.

Book rental schemes, in which books owned by the state or school are lent to students for the school year on payment of a fee, reduce the cost to families because the cost of the books can be amortized over three or more years. It is possible, moreover, to allocate funds to the schools so they can buy textbooks and learning materials through local booksellers, thus supporting the retail part of the book chain. The system is a compromise between state purchase and family purchase with benefits of both, but requires durable books, safe storage between school years and educational staff trained to handle money, manage stock and supervise loans.

It works only if the fees go into a revolving fund, the fund is used only to replace worn-out or obsolete materials, the books last as long as expected, teachers and children are trained in book care and repair, few copies are lost or stolen, book prices and enrolments do not rise abruptly, revisions to the curriculum are not too frequent and families can pay the rental fee. The system is usually cost-effective, given that the cost of a book that will last for three to five years is probably no more than 50 per cent greater than the cost of the same book produced with poorer paper and binding that will last only one year.

However, book rental was found to be a less than perfect solution in a study of representative primary-level public schools, urban and rural, in Guinea. Only 32 per cent of the books available in the schools were actually rented to pupils. Most of the pupils came from poor families, or families that were illiterate in French.

The parents already had to spend money for exercise books, pencils and other school expenses, all at the beginning of the school year. Some parents were reluctant to spend a substantial amount of money for books that might be lost or damaged by their children.

Problems have also arisen with late payment of fees and accountability in financial management, as reported, inter alia, in a forthcoming ADEA publication, Financing Textbooks and Training Materials in Africa. One consultant with considerable international experience suggests that revolving funds work best in small discrete communities where the disbursement and accounting pathways are relatively short, as at the school or local level or in small island nation. Once again, the government can reduce the cost to families, this time by annual grants to the revolving fund.

Many projects in support of textbook provision have subsidized the supplier usually the government in ways that have either reinforced a state monopoly or distorted the market. Subsidies for production, whether in cash or in materials such as paper, tend to mask the real costs of production. Unless special care is taken, they result in prices that cannot be maintained if external assistance ends. They can help to solve short-term problems if applied with care, but may have no positive long-term results. In general, subsidies should be applied only to the one-time costs that are incurred before printing begins.

Subsidization of state monopolies has usually in the past reinforced the monopoly without building sustainability.

Subsidization of individual (possibly state-owned or parastatal) publishers in a competitive market has given the recipients a competitive advantage and discouraged the entry of other publishers.

Subsidizing the supplier may, moreover, prove ineffective if the subsidy is inadequate. Read reports that in one country where books were sold, supply-side subsidies succeeded in reducing the cost of the textbooks by half, but sales did not increase; the books had simply been made cheaper for the elite who could afford them already.

Increasingly, funders are turning to demand-side subsidies as a more effective way to assist in the provision of textbooks. The subsidization becomes more effective the further down the education ladder it reaches. Direct subsidies to parents or pupils help to keep the cost to them of textbooks low and open opportunities for competition among publishers without creating market distortions. If it is impractical to provide subsidise to families, the money may be given to individual schools; and if that is impossible, selection can be placed in the hands of the schools even if the responsibility for finances and procurement is at a higher level.

Under a scheme supported by the International Development Association, for example, stipends are paid to young women in Bangladesh who are preparing for the secondary school certificate. Education among women in Bangladesh is among the lowest in the world and access to the examination had been restricted to those who could afford examination fees, stationery and private tutoring. The stipend includes a book allowance and also covers tuition, school fees, uniforms, shoes, umbrellas, transportation and other costs.

Stipends are paid twice a year into bank accounts in the names of the students, who thus also learn to manage money. Parents must agree that their daughters will attend school for at least 75 per cent of the school year, a condition that recognizes that about 90 per cent of rural girls work as household helpers. The students must obtain at least second-class marks and remain unmarried until they earn the secondary school certificate. A similar scheme is under way in Guatemala.

Alternatively, supply-side subsidies are being targeted directly to disadvantaged populations. The development of local-language textbooks for minority groups in China and Mexico was mentioned in Part III.

In both the Philippines and Bangladesh, ADB is funding textbook provision only in the poorest provinces, leaving it to the national government to fund free provision elsewhere in the country. Namibia introduced a policy of positive discrimination in 1998 under which it provides textbooks, posters, maps, wall charts and encyclopedias to disadvantaged schools.

Advances have been made in respect to gender equity and sensitivity to minority groups, but much remains to be done. Some ministries of education have established social content guidelines for the authors, publishers and evaluators of textbooks. Even when efforts are made, however, stereotypes slip past.

In Zambia, textbook writers included many examples of role reversal and balance, and female assertiveness. But in one book a man and a woman are still seen introducing themselves by saying 'I am a man' and 'I am a woman', the man with his hands hanging freely at the side, the woman with hands cupped in a posture of general deference.

The provision of textbooks in local languages is a matter of pedagogical as well as social concern, for programmes that teach people in their own language have been proved to be more effective in both Latin America and Africa than those using the language of a former colonial power. Where local languages are extensively used, as Hausa is in Nigeria, the economics of local language publication are manageable.

For small language groups, the problems are more formidable because the print runs are so much smaller.

There may be additional difficulties in securing type faces for special scripts, or in agreement on orthography, or in finding writers and editors with the requisite knowledge of subject and language. There is, however, considerable scope for South-South cooperation, building on experience in the Pacific and elsewhere, and in the late 1990s there has been renewed interest in Africa in publishing in cross-border languages.

FUNCTIONS OF A GUIDE

In the concern over the inadequate provision of textbooks and learning materials, too little attention has been paid to the use of those materials and the continuing training of teachers in their use. Generally, pre-service training should be reinforced by in-service training through various channels and by school inspectors. Some countries have tried to establish resource centres to help teachers improve the learning environment in their classrooms; others have established teacher clusters to provide peer support and in-service training. Not all such initiatives have been maintained, however. When teachers fail to use books well, they deprive themselves and their pupils of a fundamental tool for promoting reading.

In particular, pre-service training in many countries fails to give due emphasis to the preparation and use of teaching and learning aids. This failure may result from lack of hours in the programme, or the inadequacy of teacher trainers in this area, or both. Creative teachers, properly trained and motivated, can overcome a lack of professionally produced materials by making their own teaching and learning aids, often with the help of the pupils or even community members. Parents do not have to be literate to participate, as long as the meaningfulness of the work is clearly explained.

Nevertheless, few teachers in the eight countries in the

UNESCO/Danida case-study survey made any effort to make teaching and learning aids, even though they seemed aware of their importance. Jamaica was the only country in which a majority of teachers made their own aids and involved children in the activity.

Locally made aids are most likely to be appropriate for the needs and experience of the children concerned. Their value does not, however, remove government's responsibility for providing both educational materials of good quality and in service training in the preparation and use of teaching and learning aids. Training programmes in future must also prepare teachers to use many forms of educational technology and techniques, both traditional and non-traditional, including electronic media, music, dance, drama, folk theatre, newspapers and games.

Teachers will also have to become increasingly aware of intellectual property rights, in particular with respect to material found on the Internet. In Africa, Asia, Latin America, and Central and Eastern Europe, teachers have proved reluctant to use new textbooks, especially those embodying new methods. Those accustomed to a jingle 'official' textbook tend to stick with it even when other books are approved and available. Human nature is essentially conservative, but is more so than normally when people are under qualified and insecure.

Where competition among textbook publishers is active and the publishers experienced, the publishers undertake the training of teachers in the use of the materials they have for sale. That is part of their marketing. Where the state is the provider and in-service training is inadequate (as it frequently is), this important stage in the introduction of new materials is too often ignored, as is constructive supervision of teachers by principals and school inspectors.

In the Republic of Korea, reluctance to use new textbooks surfaced when a new curriculum in the national language was introduced that changed the emphasis in teaching from repetition and detailed reading of set passages to speaking, listening, and writing. The single textbook in Korean that had been used at each level was replaced by a set of three and the number of pages doubled.

The change was made after wide consultation, research and pilot testing, but the teachers resisted it, complaining that they now had more content to cover without an increase in the time available. Over several years, they gradually changed their opinion and recognized the value of the new books.

That change coincided with a change in teaching methods towards individualized instruction. The experience demonstrated that it is easier to change textbooks than teachers' preferences and habit. In contrast, teachers in Kazakhstan were given intensive training in the methods incorporated in a new generation of textbooks and are reported to have welcomed the new materials with enthusiasm (UNESCO/Danida case-studies: Kazakhstan).

The parallel trends towards multiple choice in textbooks and decentralization place parallel responsibilities on the state. The first is to ensure that all the books bought with public money, or recommended by the schools for purchase by families, meet minimum standards. There must be a process of evaluation and authorization that is not only objective and thorough, but can be demonstrated to have these qualities. This in turn requires a governing board with some members from outside the Ministry of Education, a set of uniform standards, a corps of trained evaluators including teachers from different parts of the country, open invitations to submit manuscripts, procedures that guarantee anonymity in submissions and confidentiality for the names and reports of the evaluators, and full and rapid reporting to publishers.

The South African criteria for selection have been described by one publisher as often seeming arbitrary and sometimes bizarre. In the Philippines, publishers complained that approvals were not only inconsistent but that evaluators tended to reject textbooks that exceeded the minimum learning competencies.

The director of the government body that supervises evaluation admitted that evaluators were sometimes appointed through friendship rather than merit and that there had not been enough time to train them.

The second responsibility of the state is to ensure that teachers and principals who have been empowered to select books can make well-informed choices. At a minimum, each school must have a full list of the textbooks and other learning materials that have been authorized for use. If possible, the list should be annotated as a guide to teachers, especially those in remote areas that may receive few visits from publishers' representatives. The notes might point, for example, to textbooks specially designed for rural schools or for the needs of minority groups. Teachers and principals (who may have the final say in any selection) must be provided with suggested criteria for choosing among textbooks and the skills of selection should become a regular part of in-service training and the training of new teachers.

Experience suggests that this is the point at which devolution of selection breaks down, especially when the transition from monopoly to choice is abrupt. Teachers who are accustomed to a single textbook throughout their career, and who may be poorly qualified in many of the subjects they teach, are ill prepared for this new responsibility. Where educational structures have traditionally been hierarchical, teachers and principals tend to be influenced in their selection by their superiors. There is no evidence that any country undergoing liberalization has adequately met the challenge.

Under state provision, the preparation and publishing of textbooks cannot be abruptly devolved from the central administration to regional or provincial offices without taking into account local capacities. In Ethiopia, under a new policy of decentralization, regional educational bureau were given the mandate for developing new primary-level textbooks.

Few regions had the trained staff to produce camera-ready copy or the printing capacity to produce the books. As a result, all regions except the national capital returned the production of English-language textbooks to the Institute of Curriculum Development and Research, which in turn had a British adviser do most of the writing. In other subjects, in general, one textbook was written centrally and translated into the ten other languages of instruction. This in effect neutralized the expected benefits of local preparation and production. The books were all printed in Addis Ababa.

COMPLICATION IN MARKETING

The physical difficulties of distribution of textbooks to the schools will not disappear. It will always be arduous and expensive to reach remote areas. In urban areas where access is easy and the market is large and concentrated, distribution is estimated to account for 25 to 30 per cent of the cost of a textbook; in remote areas, distribution may cost twice as much as the textbook itself.

In many countries where the state is responsible for distribution, public funds have proved inadequate to the task. The last part of the journey, from district or regional warehouses, has usually been left to the initiative of individuals' inspectors, principals, teachers and parents using whatever means of transportation are available.

The Discrepancies in the Textbook: Pupil ratio between urban and rural schools throughout much of the world testify to the failures of the system. Occasionally, the army has carried books to remote areas by helicopter. Distribution by the state has been hampered as well by human failings that should be amenable to improvement. Books have been damaged because they were inadequately wrapped or stored in insecure locations. Systems for estimating needs, accounting for inventory and recording shipments have been poorly designed or maintained.

Consolidation of orders for economy has resulted in delays when one title of several was late in delivery. Books have been slipped from central warehouses months after the school year began because there was not enough staff or money to do better. Large-scale textbook projects have not always allowed adequately for the recurrent costs of distribution. Some of these problems can be reduced by decentralizing book procurement.

Distribution through the private sector faces many of these hurdles and is further hindered by the lack of retail outlets in rural areas. Supplementary materials will be stocked only selectively, because few shop owners have the capital to hold large inventories of slow-selling goods. If there is sufficient profit to be made, however, retail outlets will spread not necessarily bookshops, more likely shops that sell stationery and other dry goods that would, for a few months of the year, stock textbooks promising a rapid turnover and relatively stable market. The ubiquity of certain soft drinks proves that profitable goods will find even the most remote markets.

The editors of a recent World Bank publication on curbing corruption observe that 'corruption is a pervasive phenomenon that can be found in countries of widely varying ideology economic conditions and social development.' They continue: Although some societies may be more vulnerable than others and may suffer more devastating effects, no country in the world today is immune from corruption's corrosive influence. Yet for all its seeming prevalence, there is no clear evidence that corruption has become more widespread today. It has been around, in one form or another, from the earliest days of social organization. What has changed is that information about corrupt practices has become more available as governments have been increasingly unable to conceal evidence of wrongdoing; the level of public tolerance for corruption has declined; and the spread of democracy seems to afford less fertile ground in which corruption can flourish.

They go on to say that malfeasance, in general, is most likely to occur where the public and private sectors meet, as they do in public procurement, contracting and licensing activities that relate directly to textbooks and other materials used in government- supported schools. Those who award contracts or procure goods may demand bribes, kickbacks, percentages or other 'gifts' from those seeking government business and sales. At a more petty level, underpaid and greedy civil servants demand their own bribes and in turn must often pay their superiors for the privilege of holding public office.

This should come as no surprise, but the potential for corruption in providing learning materials may astonish even a nation accustomed to abuses of power. After the private sector took over the provision of learning materials to the public schools of the Philippines in 1998, the newspapers carried sensational stories of bribery and misuse of funds, involving all levels of government from minor clerks to congressmen and, in one instance, the office of the President. Increased funding for learning materials has simply increased the amount of bribery, according to the reports.

Funds were diverted from textbooks to supplementary materials that carry a higher mark-up and a higher rate of bribery, despite declining textbook: pupil ratios. A new undersecretary of education has instituted various internal controls and stringent bidding procedures that he predicts will double the number of books for the country's public schools, but he admits that no system is entirely foolproof and some abuses will occur.

Abuse of another kind occurs when a cartel of suppliers

forces the government to negotiate with it for want of any other source of goods. This happened in Bangladesh, where the textbooks for government schools were produced by more than 400 small printers. The government adopted an open bidding procedure to meet funder's requirements, but ultimately acceded to the cartel because no single member of it could produce all the country's needs alone. Printers who have large and largely under-used web presses do not bid for textbooks for fear of industrial action by the small printers that would close them down.

The President of Transparency International suggests four types of strategy to reduce corruption. The first is to work within the underlying structure of government programmes and focus on improving government integrity, enforcing the existing law, designing effective penalties for bribers and bribe-takers, and developing international support mechanisms. The second is to reform the procedural basis of government to increase transparency and discourage corruption.

The third is to address government programmes that may give rise to corruption because they are poorly designed or unnecessary for example, by standardizing specifications, limiting discretion of civil servants and establishing new public-interest criteria for bidding. The fourth is to encourage self-regulation within the private sector and changes in public attitudes concerning accountability and transparency.

The International Commission on Education for the Twenty-first Century argued that one of the main aims of educational reform should be to involve stakeholders in decision-making. Decentralization, it said, would encourage innovation and participation by all. It would also allow further consideration to be given to the cultural and linguistic aspirations of minority groups and it could enhance the relevance of education through carefully worked out appropriate programmes.

It has been suggested that funds generally are used more

efficiently the closer decision-making is to the actual user of the material. O'Connor argues that corruption is inevitable when there is only one customer for textbooks, as in centralized procurement by the state: 'The most effective influence on the purchase decision of a sole customer is not quality of product or value for money but the size of a more or less overt 'commission' to persons of influence... All textbooks publishers, both indigenous and international, in countries where centralized textbook approval and purchasing systems operate are compelled to adopt these practices... they cannot do otherwise; it is a matter of marketplace survival, not business ethics.'

She agrees that the most positive effects of donor provided textbooks seem to occur when the process of selection is at the lowest possible rung of the education system. Parents' associations can act as watchdogs to ensure that money allocated to schools is spent appropriately and in response to the community's needs.

In Bolivia, for example, community participation and decentralization are considered essential parts of the national educational reform, not only to encourage respect for cultural diversity and multilingual education, but also to help curb corruptions by providing a channel for social censure. The school community has been involved in demand-side financing of textbook provision in Armenia and Guinea, helping to decide which families or students are neediest and should receive financial assistance. A similar strategy has been proposed in Cambodia.

Decentralization is far from a perfect answer, of course. Brick-hill and Priestley recognize that, especially in rural areas, books and reading are not part of the social and cultural life, which may limit the effectiveness of local surveillance of book acquisitions. Pope warns that efforts to reduce corruption by decentralizing can backfire badly unless a strong and honest team is appointed to oversee and audit public procurement. Even the strongest advocates of stakeholder participation acknowledge that civil society is a player in corruption, although it is also the major victim.

But Kisubi, a former senior adviser to the Ministry of Public Works in Uganda, argues that where genuine anti-corruption attempts have failed, one ingredient has invariably been missing, and that is the involvement of civil society. Any attempt to develop an anti-corruption strategy that neglects fully to involve civil society, he says, is neglecting one of the most potentially useful tools available.

FUNDAMENTAL REQUIREMENTS

Everything that has been learned from experience with textbooks applies also to the other kinds of learning materials. Indeed, even more vigilance may be necessary because of the wide range of supplementary materials and the much more limited resources available to buy them.

The benefits of careful planning in the purchase of books for school libraries has been demonstrated in Bolivia. The country has 32 languages, of which 3 are major. In 1995, it began building classroom and school libraries for 11,000 urban and rural schools and for 1,800 resource centres where teachers could be trained and exchange information.

Each classroom library under the scheme contains 45 titles, one-third of them produced locally. Each school library contains 10 reference books and each resource centre, 150 titles. In all, nearly 6.5 million books were acquired through competitive bidding. Procurement followed several stages. A year before bidding was announced, the Ministry of Education made contact with more than 100 publishing houses in the Spanish-speaking world. In response to the call for bids, 120 publishing houses from 16 countries submitted proposals. About 5,000 sample books were received and reviewed by 50 readers, all classroom teachers. After six months, 798 books were selected for further review, this time by schoolchildren, parents and teachers at book fairs in three regions.

The number of selected titles was winnowed to 730, at which point their 51 publishers were asked to submit prices. Ultimately, 370 titles from 48 publishers were bought in quantities of 1,800 to 22,000 copies. About one-tenth of the titles were translations from Spanish into one of the main indigenous languages. To ensure that a reasonable number of Bolivian authors would be included, the Ministry organized a national literary contest, paid for first-time rights to the 123 winning manuscripts and edited them for publication.

The value of Bolivia's multi-stage strategy can be seen by comparing its results to similar projects in Chile, where only 16 publishers participated, and in Peru, where 24 did. School libraries are expensive to build and maintain. They require basic storage facilities, pre-service and in-service training of teacher-librarians, and efficient systems of distribution, management, inspection and supervision. Book box libraries have proved more cost-effective in some projects.

National agencies have been started in some countries to direct and assist the development of school libraries by providing training, books and advice. These school library services began in Africa with independence but, despite initial enthusiasm for the concept, they have failed to maintain their early promise.

The activities of those that were established in Ghana, the United Republic of Tanzania, and Nigeria declined; in some other countries, a service was planned but never came into being. Finances have been blamed for the failure, but indifference was also a factor.

In oil-rich Nigeria of the 1980s, for example, money went to tertiary-level libraries but not to school libraries. School library services that were located in the National Library rather than the Ministry of Education proved less effective because they did not have the strong support of educational administrators. Others failed because they did not gain the support of teachers, who did not recognize the value of libraries and who were focused on formal instruction based on the textbook.

Computers and other instruments that are common in the industrialized countries are beyond the budgets and the infrastructure of much of the world. The use of new educational technologies normally depends on reliable, high quality telecommunications connections, which are seldom found in developing countries. Even where they are available, the countries may lack the necessary pedagogical and technical support to implement programmes successfully. Many respondents to the AREA/ UNESCO survey dismissed non print media as irrelevant while textbooks and other basic learning materials remain scarce.

The lessons taught in school will dissipate if there nothing to support them outside the classroom. Continuing literacy requires a literate community, which in turn will enable people to continue learning. The availability of books and other printed material leads to social and political awareness and to continuous self-learning in practical matters such as health, nutrition, agricultural practices and small business operations. In countries in which the book trade has been destroyed by war or economic collapse, in many countries of Africa, and in remote regions everywhere, the need is great.

Henry Chakava, a distinguished Kenyan publisher, has said that 'There is talk in the North about a 'bookless' society, meaning a post-book society, while for us in Africa 'bookless' societies are indeed 'pre-book societies.' It is difficult with donor funding to increase access to written materials in everyday life, but funding agencies and civil society organizations are making the effort.

The Swedish International Development Cooperation Authority (Silo) has had a broad programme for support of a literate environment, ranging from the supply of Braille presses to workshops for writers of literacy materials and the development and production of supplementary readers, science kits and radio programmes. It has supported the various links in the book chain, from the collection and publication of oral literature, through writing and publishing, to promotional events such as book weeks and book fairs.

It has helped to fund libraries and reading rooms in Botswana, Ethiopia, Mozambique, Nicaragua and the United Republic of Tanzania, language projects in Sierra Leone, Zimbabwe, the Lao People's Democratic Republic and Panama, and authors and authors' organizations such as PEN International.

It has bought and distributed children's books, and has supported libraries, reading campaigns and the training of librarians and teachers in Gaza and the West Bank. It has also supported adult literacy and post-literacy classes, often with accompanying assistance to village reading rooms, rural newspapers, and other materials for new-literates.

The Children's Book Project in the United Republic of Tanzania directly addressed the absence of books for children in a country where even textbooks in rural schools were scarce.

To encourage the development of local writing and publishing, in 1991 it launched the buy-back scheme mentioned in Part III, guaranteeing to purchase 3,000 copies of selected new children's titles if the publisher would put at east another, 2,000 copies on the open market. The 3,000 copies were distributed to rural libraries and primary schools, and their purchase was just enough to ensure the publisher a return on the initial investment; the additional copies sold would be profitable.

The project was conceived by CODE and supported by Sida, Danida, the Netherlands Embassy. The British Council, the Canada Fund and the Aga Khan Foundation. The project included training courses for writers, publishers, editors and illustrators. Ninety titles were produced by twenty-seven publishers and several were reprinted. The infusion of 270,000 books into rural areas created a demand for more. There were problems m the implementation, but a review team in 1995 recommended further support and the participating donors considered it one of the most successful publishing initiatives in Africa.

In India the Rajiv Gandhi Foundation is building networks of village libraries and stocking them with books and newspapers in the local language. The libraries are run by village committees that are responsible for providing suitable premises fox the library, identifying a librarian, and general financial management. They are expected to become financially self-sustaining through low membership fees municipal grants, and donations.

The foundation supplies initial financing, furniture, training for the librarian and a collection of about 400 books, chosen with community assistance. Efforts are made to integrate the collection with other local rural development projects, Books are lent among libraries to obtain diversity at minimum cost.

The libraries are intended to lend books for reading at home. There is not enough accommodation in most villages for reading rooms and there is concern that women might hesitate to use a reading room that becomes a place where men congregate. In Egypt, Mme Suzan Mubarak, the wife of the President, initiated a national project called 'Reading for All' in 1990, to encourage reading among schoolchildren during their summer vacation. Children win awards for reading in various subjects, competitions are held among schools, simplified low cost books are published in a 'Family Library' and mobile libraries provide access to book in remote villages.

CONTRIBUTION OF PRIVATE PUBLISHERS

Shareholders are more likely to be concerned about achieving economies and making use of professional skills than civil servants who have no personal stake in textbook provision beyond their own survival in office. Of course there are many civil servants who are just as dedicated and professional as any private-sector manager, but even they are likely to be overcome by the inertia of large bureaucracies and the indifference or unwillingness of their superiors to make changes. Publishing, in contrast to bureaucracy, benefits from a personal style that marries innovation and professionalism. It is also unusually complex in the number of 'product lines' each book constituting a separate product that must be managed simultaneously in development or revision, production, and distribution.

Because the private sector sells textbooks, either to the government or on the open market, it has funds to reinvest in the next year's sales and a powerful motivation the need for financial turnover to make that reinvestment. Books that are available this year, therefore, are likely to be available next year if the sales potential this year is realized. The difference between public and private sector publishing was illustrated dramatically in French-speaking sub-Saharan Africa, where several countries agreed on common syllabuses in mathematics and, with help from French aid organizations, cooperatively developed textbooks for common use. Two approaches to publication were followed. In the primary-level series, the intergovernmental coordinating committee that developed the books acted as publisher and retained the copyright. It offered film for plate making to countries that signed an exclusive five year agreement with it.

The countries then had to secure their over funding, by grants or loans, and arrange production of the books. The series was adopted by only three countries. In Benin, the government took three years to find funding. The state printer was given the contract for books at the first two levels but could not fulfil it for technical reasons and subcontracted it to a foreign printer at a high cost. Benin subsequently chose books for the next two levels from a French publisher. In Mali, the contracted printer delivered the books a year late. Because the financing did not cover distribution, only part of the stock was supplied to schools, mainly in the capital and its neighbourhood. The Democratic Republic of the Congo also needed three years to find funding, then chose a European printer and faced similar problems in delivery and distribution.

None of the three countries had funds to reprint books in following years. In contrast, the committee that developed the secondary-level textbooks assigned the copyright to a single publisher, the Hachette subsidiary EDICEF. The secondary series was adopted in twelve countries and sold in the open market, helped by a French subsidy to lower the sale price. About 1.5 million copies were bought, either in bookshops or within the framework of a bid, at the equivalent of US$5 per copy, about half the price of a comparable Ghanaian book, also the recipient of development aid. The books continue to be available throughout the countries because they are in the copyright of a publisher with an interest in their commercial longevity.

The foundation for a sustainable publishing industry that can meet continuing local needs while reflecting local conditions and experiences. The importance of school books extends far beyond the classroom. A large and relatively stable continuing demand for them, year after year, can provide the financial underpinning for a more general publishing industry. With the capital generated from educational books, publishers can engage in works of fiction and poetry, and in works of non-fiction books that examine the country's history, society, economy, ecology, and culture that will help to develop a sense of national identity and self-awareness.

Most important in this context, they can develop books in all these genres written specially for children and young adults, and sell them in the marketplace to a book-hungry population. In short, publishers who have financial resources from school books can provide the books that will maintain literacy once schooling ends.

Textbooks are particularly important to publishing in countries that do not have a well-developed reading culture. In industrialized countries, textbooks and learning materials represent between 25 and 50 per cent of all publishing income. In developing countries where textbooks are sold, they can represent up to 95 per cent of the local publishing market. In sub-Saharan Africa overall, they account for 75 per cent of publishing revenue.

When the state dominates the provision of learning materials, the general publishing industry languishes. This was clear in many countries of Africa and Asia, where the imposition of a state monopoly devastated publishing. As one publisher explained it, 'a book industry without access to the textbook market is a dying industry, because the textbook market is the side of the bread that is buttered for the publisher and bookseller.'

A public monopoly may appear attractive because it cuts out the retailer and concentrates production, leading to apparently lower costs for the consumer, whether that is the government or the family.

The true cost to the country is great, however, commercial publishing lacks a financial base on which to build. Bookshops do not develop because they have no books to sell. The quality of textbooks deteriorates from lack of competition.

Book industries stagnate or die. 'It is not surprising,' Brickhill and Priestley observed, 'that book development... is weakest where monopolies are strongest.' In contrast, when textbook provision is opened to commercial competition, even partially, industries grow.

Children's book production, for example, increased notably in Kenya, Nigeria and Uganda during the 1990s, in number of titles and in copies per title printed. The ownership local or foreign of commercial publishing houses that produce textbooks is not an issue so long as their publishing activity is truly locally based and locally oriented.

Locally produced books are likely to be cheaper than imported books from Europe or North America, and far more likely to be appropriate in content, illustration and emphasis.

In contrast, the foreign imported children's books the most common form of children's literature in the bookshops of many African countries have been described by Chinua Achebe as 'poisons wrapped in between beautiful covers'.

The President of the United Republic of Tanzania has said that it is 'incumbent upon African publishers to protect African value systems and ways of life'.

CONTRIBUTION OF CENTRAL GOVERNMENT

Government policies for book provision are often impeded by other government policies and practices. Not infrequently the policies of other departments impede the policies of educational authorities.

Most notable are high tariffs imposed by the Ministry of Trade or Finance on imported paper, other raw materials, printing equipment and replacement parts. Such tariffs are particularly onerous in countries that have acceded to the Florence Agreement on the free movement of books and charge no duty on imported finished books but levy high tariffs on the materials for publishing books at home.

Tariffs may be used to shield inefficient domestic paper mills as well as to raise revenue. An ADEA/APNET study on the intra-African trade in books has illustrated the contradictions in taxation and legislative practices that can work against the development of the book chain in countries committed to Education for All.

High interest rates set by the central bank also inhibit book development by commercial publishers, who may be further penalized by government subsidies to parastatal publishing and printing houses with whom they and their printers compete.

The Ministry of Culture or Education may require textbooks to be produced in two, three or even eleven local languages, a policy that is pedagogically sound but adds greatly to the investment involved in book development. The absence of intellectual property legislation, or governmental indifference to its infringements, encourage piracy of books and fragment markets that may already be marginal.

When there is no coordination among ministries in policy or regulation, the cost of providing school books generally rises. In times of fiscal austerity, that usually means that fewer books will be produced or bought, and the textbook pupil ratio grows unacceptably high.

Books cannot be considered independently but only as part of a process involving many players and policy issues. A school book is part of a continuum that begins with the students needs, as defined by a curriculum institute, and ends with the student's use, inside or outside the classroom.

In between there are many stages: curriculum development and authorization, identification and commissioning of authors, drafting and revising of a manuscript, preparation of illustrations, evaluation by the publisher in field tests, evaluation by the Ministry of Education, possible revision and further evaluation leading to authorization for use of the book in schools, production (typesetting, printing and binding) and, finally, shipping to a government warehouse and from there to individual schools or, alternatively, shipping to wholesale and retail outlets that will sell the book to families. This is not an exhaustive list of processes or players.

The World Bank or another funder may be involved, with its own procedures and guidelines which may be different from the government's development agencies and civil society organizations may supply paper or expertise.

Teachers will need training in the use of a new textbook and teachers' guides must be prepared following all the same steps simultaneously for them. Any weak links in this book chain will, as we have seen, affect the availability of books in the classroom.

The policy issues that must be examined have been set in detail by several authors. They include:

— selection of subjects requiring textbooks (core subjects or all subjects);
— use of national and local languages in instruction and textbooks; timing of reforms and revisions;
— rewards for authors;
— target textbook pupil ratios (if books are provided by the state);
— technical specifications for paper, printing and binding;
— procedures for evaluation and authorization of textbook by the Ministry of Education that are and are seen to be objective, thorough, comprehensive, fair, timely concerned with social content and in the public interest;
— affordable and sustainable financing;
— open competitive bidding for printing and/or publishing;
— practical and economical distribution;
— professional development for publishing personnel and educators;

- — identification and provision of supplementary reading and other learning materials, including their development, publication, distribution and financing;
- — support for public and school libraries, and the training of teacher librarians; and
- — positive industrial policies affecting publishing.

Failures in planning and coordination will affect the provision of textbooks and learning materials adversely. External support will be meaningful only if it is rooted in detailed strategic plans, rather than based simply on general policy statements.

Large-scale loans in the past have unquestionably reduced the pupil-to-textbook ratio in many countries from extreme scarcity to a more effective level. But book provision, as Bgoya has pointed out, is not the same as book development. Textbooks have too often been viewed as commodities to be delivered in the short run to meet immediate needs. As a World Bank team leader once remarked with passion: 'All care about is getting books into the children's hands!' If the government receiving a loan for textbook provision is still unable to fund its needs when those books must be replaced, a second loan must be negotiated.

The World Bank acknowledged, in its draft policy released in 1998, that 'many book provision efforts over the last 25 years, some with Bank support, may have achieved their immediate objectives but have been unable to maintain the service over the longer term to sustain the educational impact that textbooks help to achieve'. This has also been true of loans by the Asian Development Bank. Newton has pointed out that is not only funders that have been responsible for short-term solutions. Ministers of Education have generally been avid for the votes that come with the promise of free books in the coming year. An insistence on international competitive bidding for all contracts above a certain threshold, while understandable from the viewpoint of the funders, has exacerbated the effects of short-term provision by channelling most of the loans for textbooks out of the recipient country. Reports to APNET indicate that in book procurement programmes supported by World Bank lending, the ratio of books from local publishers to those from foreign-based publishers is 1 to 50.

A book purchase made on the basis of a one-off cost import is not a good bargain when we consider: the opportunity cost of jobs lost to the economy, since the book was not produced locally; the cost of discouraged innovative trading, which would have resulted from higher turnover and increased profitability; the cost of capacity not built; and the cost of lost spill over benefits, which in turn would have invigorated the textbook industry. As a result, these books are not cheap.

Very few governments fully understand the critical role indigenous publishers can play in national culture and, more specifically, in textbook provision, nor have they paid serious attention to the conditions that would encourage an indigenous publishing industry.

Publishers have a responsibility to raise awareness of these issues if they want change. An experienced textbook publisher, now a consultant, recommended to the Canadian International Development Agency that any project related to educational books be preceded by an in-depth analysis of the book sector; be designed to cover a minimum of ten, and preferably fifteen, years; be coordinated with other agencies; view textbook provision within an overall framework of developing local capacities in publishing, production and distribution; give priority to financial sustainability and substantial private sector involvement; and use experts in curriculum development, publishing, production and distribution in the project's planning, implementation, monitoring and evaluation.

Foundation's principles for support of the book sector show the same holistic approach: using the commercial potential of a book wherever possible to keep subsidies to a minimum and to provide an incentive for efficiency; leaving as much initiative as possible to the publishers; avoiding monopolies; and making support part of an educational process that aims at reducing dependence on external help through carefully focused training and business planning. These are desiderata that any funding agency should consider.

CONTRIBUTION OF STATE GOVERNMENTS

The state has the initiative and ultimate responsibility for the timely and adequate provision of textbooks in any publicly funded education system. It decides what textbooks will be used, how they will be published and how they will be paid for. These responsibilities remain even when some functions are performed by the private sector. The International

Commission on Education for the Twenty-first Century defined the state's role as follows:

> Education is a collective asset that cannot be left only to market forces. Thus, whatever the organization or degree of centralization or diversification of a system, the state must assume certain responsibilities to its citizens, . . .
>
> That role . . . must not, however, be exercised as a strict monopoly. It is more a matter of channelling energies, promoting initiatives and providing the conditions in which new synergies can emerge. It is also a matter of insisting on equity and quality in education . . . . more specifically, the state should play a re-distributive role, to the benefit of minorities and the underprivileged especially. Guaranteed educational quality moreover implies the establishment of general standards and various monitoring devices.

Ingemar Gustafsson, then head of Sida's education division,

defined a further public responsibility, to ensure that textbooks reflect the culture of the student-users' own country. This in turn requires each country to have some control over and capacity to produce its own school books.

At a minimum, the state must be expected to prepare clear and detailed curriculum guidelines; make them available for the development of textbooks; establish an objective process of evaluation and authorization of textbooks; decide the channels to be used in funding and distributing textbooks to the schools; set minimum physical standards of production; perform the same functions with respect to other learning materials, including teachers' guides and supplementary reading; train teachers in the use and care of textbooks and learning materials; and protect intellectual property rights through appropriate legislation.

The state may also be expected to support libraries and promote literacy through community-based campaigns. Beyond this, the state may play a role in any of the permutations outlined by Searle and described in the preceding pages. Experience suggests that no option is perfect and that what is best for one country may be unsuitable for another.

Too often, inexperienced managers and editors ignore ways to save money in textbook printing that are standard practice among trained professionals. The size of a book's page can have surprising implications for its cost, especially when paper represents a high proportion of total production expenditures.

The most economical page size is determined by the size of the sheet of paper used in printing, which in turn is related to the size of the printing press being used. Any mismatch between press and sheet, or between sheet size and page size, results in waste.

Production costs can also be reduced by restricting the number and size of illustrations, the use of colours other than black, and the total number of pages. More generally, governments can reduce costs to state and families by limiting the number and size of textbooks required.

DOUBLE EFFORTS

Privatization has been successful in providing a long-term supply of textbooks. Where the government opted for a system of purchase by families at both primary and secondary levels and concentrated production in a very few hands. In 1991 the country's two textbook publishers, le Centre edition et distribution africain (CEDA) and les Nouvelles editions ivoiriennes (NEI), both parastatal partnerships between the government and French publishers, were technically bankrupt following an economic crisis and social disorder. In order to obtain new capital they were transformed into private companies.

In both, the government retained 20 per cent of the shares and further shares were set aside for individual Ivorians to ensure majority local control. The balance of NEI shares was held by three French companies and the balance of CEDA shares by one French and one Canadian company. The new companies were granted exclusive rights, shared equally between them, to publish primary school textbooks, teachers' guides and work books, all written in the Ministry of Education. The two companies are also active at the secondary level, where the state issues a list of approved textbooks.

The state regulates the retail prices of textbooks and in the first two years of the agreement negotiated substantial decreases; prices were frozen even after the devaluation of the CFA franc increased the cost of imported materials substantially.

The price of textbooks to disadvantaged areas is subsidized. Through its share holding and regulation, including quality control, the state acts as 'school protector' while remaining committed to economic liberalism. The results of the Ivorian policy are substantial. Textbook prices are said to be the lowest in all French-speaking Africa, except where prices are artificially lowered by external subsidies.

The two national publishers sell more than 4 million primary school books each year for a school population of about 1.5 million students, and there is an additional market in second hand books. It is estimated that 75 to 95 per cent of students, depending on their level and where they live, own French and mathematics textbooks, although fewer own books in other disciplines. The system has encouraged the development of the only major printing industry in French- speaking sub-Saharan Africa and of a distribution network of wholesalers, bookstores and other sales outlets. The companies have returned profits. The World Bank is supporting free distribution of the textbooks in 116 marginalized zones.

The Ivorian policy is based on a single textbook for each subject/level. The quality of a textbook determines how well the needs of the users are met and a good quality textbook in a single-textbook system is probably better than several competing textbooks of poor quality. Many educators and publishers argue, however, that a multi-textbook system is preferable because competition encourages publishers to innovate and improve their textbooks and teachers' guides.

Gaston de Bedout, a Colombian commercial publisher, presents another reason for moving away from a single compulsory textbook in each subject, whether published by the government or bought by the government from a friendly publisher. In the final analysis, 'education through a texto unico will result in a mass of people desolately uniform, indoctrinated by the official history, philosophy, science, grammar, chemistry, biology, and even the official calligraphy.

Personnel must be trained in manuscript development, editing, design, illustration, field testing, production control, marketing, warehousing and distribution. Authors must be identified and they too must be trained to meet the special demands of writing textbooks and teachers' guides. Training tended during the 1990s to focus on the more obvious needs of writing, editing, design and illustration. Less attention was paid to preparing publishers for the underpinning skills of operational and financial management, marketing, and evaluation' an imbalance that is gradually being redressed.

Typically, a textbook takes three years from inception to the classroom roughly, one year or more to commission authors and for them to write a first draft; one year for field testing, revision and evaluation by the Ministry of Education for authorization; one year to produce final books and, especially where distribution is difficult, get them to the schools. The process can be accelerated, but only if the commercial sector is sufficiently established to meet the challenge.

It can be impeded by difficulties in securing capital or credit and, too often during liberalization, by bureaucratic foot dragging. Uganda's experience illustrates the time an industry takes to develop. Up to 1993, the National Curriculum Development Centre had a monopoly on textbook production and the few books it produced were assigned to two transnational publishers.

Other textbooks bought under a World Bank project were all imported. In 1993 the centre's monopoly was removed and selection was devolved to the schools, choosing from a centrally approved list. By the end of the decade, ten publishers were sharing the market.

A result of a general government policy of economic liberalization, lobbying by a newly formed book publishers' association and pressure from the principal funder of a primary-level textbook provision scheme, the United States Agency for International Aid (USAID).

About US$20 million was spent under the project between 1993 and 1997 and publishers responded with vigour. Sales representatives combed the countryside, visiting schools and addressing teachers' meetings no easy job in a country with more than 8,000 government-aided primary schools, many of them in remote areas with poor roads.

Local publishers built sales and skills. Some mutually beneficial joint ventures developed with foreign partners. The quality of textbooks improved. Publishers from abroad set up offices employing local people. Bookshops expanded from five in Kampala in 1990 to twenty-five and others upcountry publishers met teachers directly to offer guidance in the use of their books.

The Ugandan book chain is developing, but its local base even after more than half a decade of such activity is still narrow. The number of local publishers is small, and the sales of textbooks have not yet been matched in other kinds of books. More than 90 per cent of the primary-level textbooks are still published by British-based transnationals who have local partners that are basically only marketing agents. Most of the printing is done abroad, because local printers lack the capacity and' in a chicken-and-egg situation' cannot afford to build capacity without the lucrative textbook jobs. The government still procures textbooks centrally, consolidating orders from the various schools, and delivers them to the schools free of charge. As a result, bookstores reap no benefits, nor does the infrastructure for general publishing.

Local publishers find it difficult to obtain credit because banks are reluctant to lend money to businesses with only one customer, even if it is a government ministry. After six years of rapid development, the book sector is still heavily dependent on external inputs. Without any attempt at cost recovery, the provision of primary-level textbooks remains dependent on external funding.

The Ugandan experience is not atypical. Publishing is not an industry that can be jump-started. Capital is a particularly high barrier to local publishing development and there have been several suggestions that governments guarantee loans to publishers, as in the Dag Hammarskjold scheme, or extend cheap credit to publishers as many do to farmers for the purchase of seeds and machinery, or obtain concessional credit for publishers through the World Bank and regional development banks. Government-guaranteed loans have proved their value in the development of the Canadian publishing industry for more than twenty years.

Zimbabwe, which has a long history of liberalization in textbooks, passed an 'import substitution' regulation in 1983 which stipulated that any textbook required in a quantity of more than 1,000 copies must be locally published. In effect, foreign publishers who wanted to tap the Zimbabwean market had to license their books to a local publisher; as a result, import expenditures were reduced and the local industry was given a powerful boost.

Mozambique, recognizing that textbook shortages were too severe to be met by local development, adopted a similar policy in 1998, under which it may authorize licensing, adaptation and co-editions of books published elsewhere, but no more than 2,000 copies of any foreign book may be imported. To meet greater demand, books must arrive under the imprint of a Mozambican publisher and/or only with special permission from the Ministry of Education. Ghana encourages joint ventures between local and foreign publishers but insists that Ghanaian authors and illustrators comprise 70 per cent of any writing team and that Ghanaian printers do 60 per cent of the printing. Still, without competition at the international level, quality can suffer. A self-sustaining but complacent local industry may fossilize, as happened in Algeria.

A transition from state monopoly to private competitive provision of textbooks cannot occur without a welcoming political climate and a clear, well-designed and open policy preferably one that has been developed in consultation with the book industry. A favourable environment for commercial publishing requires decentralization of funds (or at least purchasing authority) to enable schools to select the textbooks and other resources they want to use and buy; capacity-building of new publishers to increase choice of textbooks and competition in quality and price; an objective and open system for approving textbooks for purchase; training in assessment, selection and purchasing of textbooks for school administrators and teachers; adequate information systems for procurement of textbooks; and effective commercial distribution systems.

The same authors argue that a multi-textbook system can be completely successful only if book purchasing is done at the lowest level and if all the books that are approved have an equal opportunity to be purchased.

When one publisher dominates the market, the second condition cannot be met. This has happened when the state continues to produce textbooks through a commercialized parastatal that may enjoy special benefits, such as subsidies or access to subsidized government printing, in competition with small private publishers who have difficulty in obtaining credit and raw materials. This situation has occurred in many countries of Eastern and Central Europe and in some countries of Africa.

Even when the state withdraws from publishing, the field will not necessarily be level. If local commercial publishers are unprepared to deliver textbooks in sufficient quantity and quality, transnational publishers will be quick to fill demand, as in Uganda.

Countries that use a metropolitan language for instruction are especially open to transnational domination. 'Ultimately, it will be simply a matter of who is able to develop, publish, and place the manuscripts on the market more quickly'.

Nine

SIGNIFICANCE OF WRITING

During teaching of a language, we develop a number of skills in our students. Writing is one of those communication skills. Through writing, a person is able to convey his thoughts or ideas to others who are not present in front of the writer. Moreover, writing makes the record permanent. Whatever is written once remains for ever; unless it is knowingly destroyed. While writing, a person has to be very exact.

In some of the institutions, it is found that too much emphasis is laid down on writing and oral aspect of the language is neglected. No doubt, this type of practice helps the learners in the present day type of examinations but it does not help them in the long run. So the different aspects of language learning should be given due importance.

Teaching how to write involves manual skill-the skill of controlling the small muscles of the fingers, and the wrist and securing coordination of the hand and the eye. Secondly, it involves doing various exercises in written work. The exercises cover a vast field ranging from copying the phrases and sentences to composing a long essay.

There are two types of learners who can be taught writing of English language. The first category is of those who have not learnt the writing of any language. The second category is of those who have already learnt the writing of mother tongue. In the first case, the teacher has to explain the learners how the have to sit, how to hold a note book in hand and how to hold a pen.

After this, they are given preliminary practice of writing with a pen. Then they are given this type of practice with the help of chalks and small boards which are meant for the students. There are blackboard boards fixed up on the four walls of the class room and they are very near to the floor on which the students are sitting. By using two type of blackboards, the students may be given practice of drawing straight lines. In the beginning, the lines may not be straight. By and by, they should be given practice in drawing short lines, in one direction and then in another direction.

After this they should be given practice in drawing circles, semi-circles etc. This type of practice should continue as long as the students are able to move their fingers and wrists according to the writing specimens. It will be all the more useful if the students are asked to study drawing as a compulsory subject at this stage. All that will be fully helpful in the learning of writing. This much practice will pave way for teaching the writing of alphabets. The second category of students who have already learnt the writing of mother tongue, are already at this stage when writing of English alphabets is introduced to them.

WRITING COUNSEL

While teaching writing, the teacher should not start from a, b, c, and go upto z. The alphabets are taught according to the convenience of the learners so that they may not face any problem all of a sudden and above all, their interest in learning is also kept in mind.

Letters, capital and small: Capital letters should be taught first because they are easy for the small children. The small letters should be taught afterwards.

While teaching capital letters, it will be more convenient if the different letters are taught category wise. First of all those letters should be taught which can be written with one or two strokes e.g. 1, L, T. Y. X, V etc. Then the letters with three strokes, four strokes and so on, can be taken up, e.g.

Handwriting styles: Gradually letters which are written with circle or semi-circle and letters with strokes and circles should be taught.

Freeman in his book: 'Teaching of Handwriting' recommends the following six groups:

(i) i, u, w,

(ii) n, m, v, x,

(iii) a, e, o. c,

(iv) r, s,

(v) d, p, q, t,

(vi) i, b, h, i, g, y, z, f

Alice E, Stephens has suggested the following groups:-

First groups involves the stroke from top to bottom:-

i, n, t, p, w, v, in, n, r.

Second group implies a round stroke as

or a, d, c, e, q,

Third group includes loops as:

b, f, y, i, k, i, z.

Fourth group is as under:

s, x.

For capital letters, F.G. French has suggested the following groups:

Round Capitals (each filling one circle)

O, Q, C, D, G.

Square Capital (each filling one square)

H, N, M, T, Z, A, X, U, T. W.

Half square Capitals (each filling half a square)

F, E, L, X, L I.

Half circle

S, P, B, R.

The above said groups are the suggestions of the different experts. Further it depends upon the individual teacher that he may form certain groups out of the alphabets depending upon the teachability of the letters or their learnability.

Different Techniques

By over writing: The teacher writes something with a pencil on the note-books of the students. The students are asked to overwrite it. It can also be done by prescribing English writing note books in which letters or words or sentences are written with dots. In this way, the students can have overwriting practice.

With the help of flash cards: Something is written on the flash cards and they are given to the students. By consulting the flash cards, the students write down the same thing in their note books.

With the help of blackboard: Something is written on the blackboard. Then the students are asked to observe it carefully and copy it down in their note books.

By teacher himself: The teacher writes the first line in the note books of the students. Then the students are asked to complete the whole page by consulting the first line.

By using substitution table: The teacher prepares a substitution table on the blackboard or on a chart. He makes them understand how they have to consult it for speaking or writing purpose.

By and by the teacher is to enable the students to write

without consulting the book flash cards or the blackboard. The teacher should see that the students have good hand writing.

Very often, it is found that the students have poor handwriting. It is first and foremost duty of a language teacher that he should help the students have good handwriting. By good handwriting, we mean legible writing which is clear to others. It does not mean decorated one.

THE PROGRESS

Writing is one of the important skills in the teaching learning of the language. Good handwriting is an asset with the learner. By good handwriting, people understand differently. Some people say that good handwriting is very beautiful to look at. It is full of ornamentations throughout. An intelligent person interprets good handwriting in another way.

By this, he means legible writing. That writing which does not strain the mind of the reader. The reader can read it easily, nicely and fluently. Some people say that handwriting is linked with the mental efficiency of a person. Surely good handwriting is the replica of one aspect of the personality of an individual.

Good handwriting makes the learner good. The learner of the language is called poor with bad handwriting. Therefore, every teacher of English must have attractive handwriting. It is all the more essential for the teacher who teaches the, beginners. Both the teacher and the learner should aim at having good handwriting. Simultaneously, the speed of writing should be maintained.

THE ILLUSTRATION

A good handwriting is a composite of some characteristics. To know about the characteristics of good handwriting is an interesting process. Let us, therefore, visualise the main characteristics of good handwriting.

The following are the characteristics of good handwriting:

Distinctiveness: Every letter of a word is distinct. It is clearly visible. It can be recognised easily by every type of learner of the language. Thus each letter is joined with the neighbouring letters of a word.

Proper spacing: There is proper space between the different words of a sentence. Whenever a new paragraph is started, some space is left. That is maintained throughout the writing. Some space is also left while starting a new sentence.

Size of the letters: The size of the letters is according to the age group of the learner. It is neither too big nor too small. The same proportion is kept in the whole writing.

Simplicity: A good handwriting is simple to look at. The different letters of a word are written in a simple way. There are no unnecessary strokes.

Straight lines: Good handwriting runs in straight lines. That is all parallel to the top of the page.

Principle of four lined note book: The principle of writing on a four lined notebook is always kept in mind. That gives uniformity to the writing.

Position of letters: While writing, the position of letters is very important. The letters may be in erect positions. They may also be in forward slant positions. Backward slant positions are to be avoided.

Good punctuation marks: Good punctuation marks are also essential in writing beautifully. The punctuation should be correct. The shape of different signs of punctuation marks should be beautiful. They can make or mar the beauty of writing.

Significance of good handwriting: In every language, handwriting of the learners is considered very important. In fact, every student of the language is expected to have good handwriting. By good handwriting we mean legible and fully clear type of writing.

The following points show the importance of good handwriting:

1. A good handwriting impresses others, especially the reader for whom it is meant.
2. A good handwriting communicates the thoughts and ideas accurately.
3. It is easily understandable. There is no scope for any type of misunderstanding.
4. It helps in creating interest of the students in language learning. Good handwriting once acquired becomes an asset with the learner.
5. Handwriting of a person speaks to a considerable extent about the personality of an individual. Thus, from good handwriting of a person we can judge about him or her.
6. Good handwriting of an examinee motivates the examiner and thus it may ensure more credit to that student.
7. A good handwriting of a person becomes a living example for others. The students whose handwriting is very good feels it a pride. The teacher whose student has got good handwriting, considers it to be a matter of his pride and privilege.

Current position: These days, many school going children have poor handwriting. The main reasons are:

(i) Many teachers don't have good handwriting. The students imitate the writing of the teachers.

(ii) The teachers do not encourage the students for good handwriting.

(iii) Ball-pens are becoming popular day by day. The use of ballpens spoil the handwriting.

(iv) Four lined note books are used for a very limited time only.

(v) No credit is given to the students whose handwriting is very good.

Handwriting: Exercise for Improvement

(i) The teacher should give proper guidance very regularly at the early stages of learning writing. He should not let go the students according to their own desires and wishes of writing. Any sort of error committed by the child should be nipped in the bud.

(ii) The teacher's writing should be a model one for the students. When he is writing on the blackboard, the students should be asked to watch his movements of hand and fingers.

(iii) Then the students should be asked to copy down the matter from the blackboard. If the teacher so feels, he may write the first line of a page in the note books of the students and ask them to complete the full page by looking at the first line. And if needed, note books in which writing is done with dots may be prescribed and the students are asked to overwrite it.

(iv) There should be frequent competitions of good handwriting. The winners may be given prizes.

(v) Good handwriting of students should be displayed in the class room. It will help improve the handwriting of other students.

(vi) At the early stages, the students should be encouraged to make use of four-lined note books. The use of fountain pen should be discouraged.

Good handwriting is very essential for every student. Both the teacher and the students should make efforts for it. The above explained methods can work wonders in improving the handwriting of school going children. The school authorities should also give importance to good handwriting. Good handwriting of the students will also have its impact on the personalities of the students.

In the teaching of writing, there is one big problem which is confronted by the learners of English language. The problem is of English spellings.

Correct Spellings: Correct spellings in every language are very important. English is not a Phonetic language. So there are more chances of committing spelling mistakes. By writing-wrong spellings, the writer can be completely misunderstood. Here under are given a few samples of writing having spelling mistakes:

1. rit (write)
2. dat (That)
3. I lowe him (I love him?)
4. Will you police sin hear. (Will you please sign here?)
5. I kame across a mankey (I came across a monkey)

By this type of writing, one can be completely misunderstood. So in the writing of a language correct spellings are very essential. In fact, correct spellings depend on the cultivation of visual memory which is an inborn quality in a person.

Schonell, F.J. writes in his book 'Backwardness in the Basic Subjects': "Spelling is a complex sensory motor process the efficiency of which is based on repeated motor reactions to sensory stimuli. In other words, mastery in spellings is possible when proper auditory and visual impressions fuse with articulatory and graphic motor responses."

Spellings in English are most irregular and illogical. The famous linguist *Max Muller* once said. "English spelling is a national misfortune to England and an international misfortune to the rest of the world." *Bernard Shaw*, the great dramatist and humourist of English has made fun of English spellings. According to him if a learner of English language has limited knowledge of words and their spelling and he is asked to write another word, there is possibility of committing blunders. He explains his point by giving an example. Suppose a person knows only three words and he makes a note of the sounds underlined in the words rough, woman, nation. Then he is asked to write the word 'Fish'. That person having limited knowledge will write it as 'ghoti'. The word 'ghoti' in place of fish is a cent percent different word. It is a jugglery of spellings in English language. The reason why spellings of English language are difficult is that it is a mixed language. Main words have been borrowed from other languages like Greek and Latin. A few examples of difficult and confusing spellings are given below:

(a) Ph is pronounced as 'F' in English. Some of the words are philosophical, photo.

(b) Ch is pronounced as 'K'. Some of the words are character, chorus.

(c) 'H' is silent in some words like hour, honour.

(d) 'K' is not sounded in some words-Knife, Knowledge.

(e) 'T' is silent in some of the words-listen, hasten.

(f) 'B' is silent in some of the words like comb, tomb.

(g) 'Gh' is not sounded in the words-bought, night, height, sight, flight, plight.

(h) 'Gh' gives the sound of 'f' in some of the words like cough, laugh, tough.

(i) Some sounds but written differently. Some of the words are way, weigh, whey.

(j) Types of errors may also include:

omissions	(wether)
additions	(waite)

insertions	(similiar)
substitution	(tence)
transposition	(recieve)
Phonetic error	(they in place of Day)

Teaching of Spellings: W.S. Tomkinson says in his book 'The Teaching of English', "Spelling is caught rather than taught. Teaching of English Spelling is not an easy job. There are different types of students and so they learn spellings in different ways. Some students are touch-minded. They learn spellings when the teacher asks them to write the spellings of the words again and again. The second category of students is called car-minded. They are able to pick up spelling when they listen to the spellings of the word. There are still other students who are called eye-minded. These students are considered to be superior to other types of students. They are able to understand spellings simply by looking at the word." So we shall have to make use of different methods for the different types of students. A few methods of teaching spellings which are commonly used, are explained here under:

1. One method of teaching spellings may be summed up 'look, say and write'. The teacher writes on the blackboard and speaks the words alongwith the spellings. Then the students speak the word alongwith spellings and copy it down in their note books.
2. Drills of different types play a significant role. Oral drill, motor drill and visual drill can be used.
3. The students may be encouraged to group together words which are almost of the same type in speaking. For example, rat, cat, bat, sat pat, etc., or tin, pin, bin, etc. This type of association exercises are useful for teaching correct spellings.
4. Different letters are written on the flash cards. They are mixed together. Then the students are asked to

frame words by using the various letters written on the flash cards.

5. The teacher writes wrong spellings of the words on the blackboard. Then the students are asked to come to the blackboard one by one and correct the spellings.
6. The commonly mis-spelt words are written on a chart and that chart is hung at some important place in the class. The students consult that chart again and again and learn spellings.
7. There are gramophone records available on which the words along with spelling are spoken. The record player is one and the students listen to the records.
8. Some interesting games may be introduced for teaching spellings. A few words are written on the blackboard. The students look at the words for some time. Then one student is asked to speak words alongwith spellings by keeping his back towards the board. It is repeated by a number of students. For this, class can also be divided into two groups and competition may be held.

Writing skills are very important for the learner of the language. Sometimes some defects are seen in the writing skills of children. A few examples of such defects are:

(a) Writing small alphabets first and afterwards learning capital letters;

(b) Backward slant in their writing;

(c) Using cursive script first;

(d) Not caring for the principle of writing on a four lined notebook;

(e) Writing carelessly and committing spelling errors.

(f) Wrong posture of sitting for writing;

(g) Wrong holding of pen, notebook etc. while writing;

All the above said defects need be fully cared for by the

learners of language from the beginning. They should see that none of these defects is allowed to linger on. These must be carefully rectified with sincere efforts. The teacher should see that small letters are taught afterwards and capital letters first because capital letters are easy in writing. The learner should be enabled to use print script first and cursive script afterwards. Principle of writing on a four lined notebook and sitting in a right posture are important and their importance should be well known to the learners of language. The learner must be discouraged in the use of backward slant in writing. Thus timely guidance and proper encouragement by the teacher must be there when the budding children are taught the skills of writing. That will equip them with good writing skills.

IMPORTANCE OF SCRIPT

In the writing of language we can have two types of scripts: (i) Print Script (ii) Cursive Script. In print script, each letter stands distinct as if in print form. But in cursive script, all the letters of a word are joined. Now the question arises which script out of these two should be followed by the beginners. The print script is suggested for them because it is more convenient for the learners. Of course, they have gradually to shift over to cursive script and they have to continue with that throughout their lives. But at the initial stages print script is useful. Given ahead are the advantages of using print script:

(i) In the books, writing is done by using print script. If the students use print script in their own writing it will be more convenient for them because they will look at the written symbols of the books exactly in the same fashion.

(ii) By using print script, the writing stands clear and distinct.

(iii) It helps in keeping the maxim of going from easy to difficult.

LANGUAGE ITEMS

The language material to be used in writing by the students should be the same which they have practised orally. Nothing new with which they are unfamiliar should be taken up for writing purposes. This will give a little bit of revision of words and structures already learnt orally. Besides, the problem of spelling is solved upto some extent.

Selection of slant: In writing, there are three types of slants: (i) backward slant, (ii) forward slant, (iii) erect position. The students should always be discouraged to use the backward slant while writing anything. The forward slant and writing in erect position are highly recommended.

Different experts of languages put forth different opinions about it. The generally accepted opinion is ..... after oral teaching, reading from blackboard or flash cards is started. In case of flash cards, those very language items are written on the blackboard in print script. When all the pupils can read those language items quickly and correctly, writing' should be introduced. During the first three or four months writing is restricted to copying. Pupils copy from the blackboard the material which they can read.

In some schools, we notice that writing is introduced alongwith reading. Moreover, they do not give any practice of listening and speaking. This is a big drawback.

Ten

SIGNIFICANCE OF READING

Any language is taught with a view to develop certain skills. The right approach to it is the natural one. Listening and speaking skills should be developed first. After giving sufficient practice of listening and speaking, then reading and writing skills should be introduced. These skills are interrelated. Good reading definitely depends upon a lot of practice in listening and speaking. If a person has learnt spoken language carefully, he will not face any problem while reading. A good speaker is always a good reader.

Bacon said, "Reading make a full man, writing an exact man." Reading skill is, undoubtedly of unique importance in the learning of a language. *A. W Frisby* says. "Reading for those who have been guided to appreciate it, is one of the most important activities of life to bring to us not only a pleasant way of spending the time, but a way of entering into the life of the world and helping us to contemplate spiritual matters. Many of those who do not approach reading in this life have probably not received in their youth the right encouragement." Thus we find that the ability to read well is very much expected from every person. *R. S. Trivedi* and *D.A. Ghanchi* write in their books 'Teaching English' .... "In fact, the education of a child is imperfect, unless he is equipped with ability to read, to decipher, to interpret and to understand properly the contents of a reading material. The intellectual advancement of a child is strictly limited if he is unable to read."

Symbol

Sound **Sense**

Reading involves recognition of sound and written symbols. Recognition of sounds is needed for listening or speaking of the language. Recognition of written symbols is important for reading purposes. Let us first of all, study what is meant by reading.

DIFFERENT KINDS

Prose may be read:

1. Loudly
2. Silently

AUDIBLE READING

Loud Reading means reading a book by producing sounds audible to others. This type of reading is useful during the first three or four cars of language learning. The reason is that the students are beginners and there is possibility of committing errors. Sometimes the learners are hesitant to reveal their shortcomings. So loud reading plays a very significant role in the teaching of a language. It is advantageous at the early stages but it will be nothing less than luxury if it is carried on at higher stages of learning the language.

Reading aloud by the teacher can help the students in the improvement of their listening ability. They are also able to sharpen their recognition of different sounds. Moreover, they can watch the movements of organs of the teacher when he is presenting model reading to the learners.

Some of the words which the students find difficult to speak are well understood by them. Pronunciation of the students is also improved considerably. So reading aloud by the teacher helps the learners in a number of ways.

Thus we find that reading aloud is of great advantage at the early stages of learning a language. According to *A. W Frisby*, "The danger of too much reading aloud as a method of teaching reading is that it may lead to the short circuiting of the meaning whereby the written word does not convey meaning but becomes merely a symbol for a collection of sounds and is translated straight in sounds."

MOCK READING

Silent reading means reading something without producing sounds audible to others. In this type of reading, the learner of language reads everything quietly. He is not expected to move his lips even. This type of reading is useful at the advanced levels of learning a language.

The reason is that at this stage the learner of language has to read a number of books. Sometime the reader is busy in reading a novel. In such cases it will be worth-while to make use of silent reading. Only then the reader will be able to go through a lot of reading material.

Silent reading is not of any use if it is carried on at the lower stages of learning a language. But at the higher stages, it is highly recommended. *A. W. Frisby* says, "While reading aloud has its uses, few pupils will have much need of it when the leave school. We must teach the skill of silent reading as soon as possible since it is useful to our pupils throughout their lives." *Handschin* states: "Silent reading inculcates love for reading and is pleasurable and it gives the pupil a feeling of power and achievement.

Silent reading is both an end and a means in reading. It is a means to achieve the following objectives:

Intellectual: The students are quickly able to get all the facts or thoughts contained in the subject matter.

Literary: The students get both entertainment and enlightenment.

Linguistic: It aims at the expansion of pupils' vocabulary.

W.S. Tomkinson very beautifully explains loud reading by distinguishing between silent reading and loud reading when he quotes two sentences (i) Culture is reading and (ii) to read well is a noble exercise by the first is meant that they should have a "technique both accurate enough to turn the print into correct sound and to tender its logical content and expressive enough to make audible the beauty or word and their emotional significance. By the second we mean reading nicely which is good and noble exercise."

Greater need of learners: Silent reading is needed by all types of learners of language whereas reading aloud is useful at specific moments alone. In general study the students will almost never be called upon to read aloud. Moreover, reading aloud prevents the students from learning to understand the meaning of a sentence even when he may not know one word in the sentence. It prevents him from doing this because he is forced to struggle with the word in order to read the sentence aloud. Reading aloud can easily be done with no comprehension at all. Allowing the students to read silently, encourages them to work for understanding rather than finishing the passage. In silent reading the students can more easily work at their own material pace or speed. Reading may be done (i) Intensively (ii) Extensively

LIMITED AND WIDE READING

Intensive reading: Intensive reading means detailed study of the passage. In this type of reading, the reader has to be careful with the different language items i.e. words, grammar, language expression, ideas etc. He tries to understand anything and everything contained in the paragraph.

Extensive reading: In extensive reading, the aim is not linguistic. Here the reader is concerned with getting the overall meaning or idea of the passage. He is not to bother about the detailed language items contained in the paragraph *W.M. River* says in his book. 'Teaching Foreign Language Skills', "The purpose of extensive programme will be to train the student to read directly and fluently in the foreign language for his own enjoyment, without the aid of the teacher."

Generally in the lower classes, books are prescribed for intensive reading. But in the higher classes, extensive reading on the part of the students is as important as is intensive reading. In intensive reading the student cannot ignore the meaning of any word. He has to follow each word or structure contained in the paragraph. But in extensive reading, he can skip over a line or a word or a structure which he fails to follow.

The prescribed books in different classes are meant for intensive reading. Read and Learn Series is a set of books prescribed for the first three years of learning English. The students here cannot ignore anything. Similarly in Prep. class, 'Poems for the Young' is a prescribed textbook for intensive reading. The students can be asked to write context and explanation in the examination. Even a critical question can be put on anything contained in the lesson.

In extensive reading, one is concerned with the over-all meanings contained in the book or chapter. Let us take up a single example. Intensive reading of a newspaper, says, 'The Tribune', That has to be done extensively otherwise one will lag far behind. Thus extensive reading breaks the dull and monotonous reading of the textbook. Moreover, the reader is not required to strain much in extensive reading.

VARIOUS KINDS

We can't say that of these two types one is better than the other and hence more important. The fact is that both these types of reading are important in their own ways. In Indian schools, we find that more stress is laid on intensive reading. The extensive reading is encouraged in a very few schools. Intensive reading should serve as a means to extensive reading.

Exercises of skimming: Skimming of a lesson means gathering together salient facts contained in it. Skimming of a prose paragraph means going through it and collecting the main points contained therein. Surely the reader is able to take out the best contained there in the lesson or the paragraph.

Practice of skimming is very important for the senior students. It gives them a lot of confidence. The main purpose of the person is to assemble main things contained therein.

Exercises of scanning: Scanning of a book or a lesson or a paragraph means collecting detailed information contained in the subject matter. The reader goes through the subject matter with searching looks. He/She examines every thing very closely. So much so that the reader is not allowed to ignore even a single difficult word contained there in. In scanning, everything good or bad is pointed out. Every thing very objectively and in a A-cry scientific manner is highlighted.

Scanning of materials is recommended for the senior students. It teaches them to call a spade a spade. It also develops the habit of working hard. It also helps them in developing scientific attitude in thinking and understanding things which is very important in life. They tend to read the subject matter cautiously and carefully.

HABITUAL GROWTH

These days, we find that the students are not in the habit of studying extra books. The, study only those books which are prescribed for the different classes. If the students continue like this, then the real aims of teaching the language will be missed. It is the duty of all concerned that they should make efforts to improve the deteriorating conditions. The examination system should also be changed.

The question paper and the syllabus expect the study of some other books. For extra reading, *Prof Rajagopalan* says: "We should concentrate all our attention on the pupils now in schools and make them more and more book-minded. We should create in them a real love for books and not only a good taste for reading."

The following steps in this direction are suggested:

(i) The teacher should explain to the students the utility of library reading. They should be given knowledge about different types of books lying in the library.

(ii) As far as possible, the books should be easily accessible to the students. For this a small library in the class-room may be started. Open shelf system may be introduced if possible.

(iii) Sometimes the teacher may tell a part of the story contained in some books. As soon as the students feel interested in it, the teacher may say that they should read the rest of the story from the books lying in the library. In such cases, it is expected that the library will have a number of copies of the book.

(iv) There should be competitions for extra reading. Thus the winners may be given prizes.

(v) In the examination, there should be some questions for which the students may be required to make use of the subject matter acquired through extra reading.

(vi) During the school hours, one period should be prescribed for library studies. It will be all the better if open-shelf system is introduced in the library.

(vii) In order to draw the attention of the students and

make them feel interested, some books of common interest may be placed in the canteen. The students in their free time will be able to have a look at them.

(viii) Sometimes there may be discussion on books and the students who show extra knowledge of books should be given either special certificates or special credit for that.

(ix) The library should have suitable type of books for all the students. There should be banks for the children, the grown ups, the teachers, the geniuses, the dullards etc.

(x) The library and the reading room should be well decorated. It will attract the readers.

(xi) The newly arrived books in the library should be notified on the notice board. If possible, the covers of those books should be exhibited on a special board meant for this purpose.

(xii) A library association of the students may be formed. The students may be involved for doing social service in the library. The students will come to know about the various books lying in the library. Thus they will be attracted towards reading some of them.

(xiii) The class teacher or the subject teacher himself should be interested in reading extra books from the library. This example of the teacher will have its effect on the students. They will also become interested in library books.

(xiv) The teacher should announce in the class the names of the students who are doing extra reading. It will give recognition to those students. Moreover, it will attract the attention of the students to library.

Thus developing the reading habits of school going children should be dealt with on priority basis.

In the words of *Prof Rajagopalan*:

> "We can never hope to improve the standard of English of our pupils and help them derive full benefits out of learning a difficult foreign language unless and until this desirable habit is formed among our students first".

THE MEANING

Reading is a process of looking at a written or printed symbol and translating it into an appropriate sound. This spoken symbol is further associated with an object for which it stands. Thus reading consists of three elements ..... the symbol (written or printed), the sound and the sense. For example, the child reads the word 'dog' in his reader. First of all, he looks at the symbol, translates it into a specific sound which stands for some animal called 'dog' and at the same time he visualises the concrete object or idea for which the said symbol stands.

Reading in fact is the ability which enables the pupils sooner or later, to read with the purpose of extracting from the printed page, the thoughts, facts and information that it has to give him. We are enlightened by reading. By reading our written message is interpreted by the other person.

Reading mechanics: When a person reads anything his eyes go on moving alongwith the printed or written symbols. If we watch carefully, the eyes do not move smoothly in one even movement. They move by jumps separated by short stops. He reads when the eyes are having a pause and not when the eyes are in movement. The number of words read in one complete movement of the eyes is called the Eye-Span.

While reading, we do not look at the various letters of a word. We rather look at the words as a whole e.g. (Chair not c-h-a-i-r) The cc span can help develop the art of reading, There are fast readers and slow readers. The reason behind it is that a fast reader has a wider eye-span, whereas a poor reader has short eye-span. While reading, some students put their fore fingers under every word. It is a bad habit because it has adverse effect on the speed of reading. So the teacher should check this bad habit at the initial stages.

THE IMPORTANCE

People generally feet that the ability to read fluently is the primary aim of learning English. Before 1900, the major aim in teaching reading was just word recognition. But in due course of time, the concept underwent a change. In the modern times, there have been many social changes and so the purposes of teaching reading have increased. So much so is the change that even the methods of teaching reading have been modified accordingly.

At present reading is taught so that a person is able:

(i) to recognise words.

(ii) to understand the meanings of words.

(iii) to react to what has been read. In other words, the child laughs, feels sad, waits for the ending etc. as the case may be. And he will disagree on false statement.

(iv) to change ideas and behaviour of the students.

Reading of mother tongue and reading of a foreign language are fundamentally the same processes. The learners face problems in both the cases. However in case of mother tongue, the problems are few because he has already learnt listening and speaking at home.

In case of a foreign language, practice in listening or speaking is given in the school. Comparatively, the learners have less practice in aural-oral aspect of the language. Besides, English is not a phonetic language. Its spelling system creates problems in reading. So it is very essential that reading should be started after giving sufficient practice in listening and speaking.

How to Begin?

Reading should not be introduced to the students unless they have acquired the ability to speak well. Now the question arises how much time should be spent for developing the speaking ability of the learners.

Thompson and *Wyatt* write in their book, 'The Teaching of English in India'. "The Indian boy is eight or nine when he begins the study of English and he can already read his mother tongue fluently... In teaching him to read English, therefore, we need not be concerned with creating in him the right attitude of mind towards the printed (or written) word."

Different linguists give different opinions about it. Some of them say that reading should be started after one year of oral practice. Some others advocate that six months oral practice is very essential.

No doubt, the opinions given by experts are based on observations made in experiments. But it is an admitted fact that we can't fix up the period for oral practice. The reason is that the period of practice will vary from place to place and from class to class. The following are the factors which determine the time to be spent on oral practice:

(i) Age of the learners.

(ii) Class in which the study of foreign language is introduced.

(iii) The ability of the students to understand and imitate the spoken language.

(iv) Ability of the teacher to maintain interest without books.

(v) The community to which the students belong.

So it is a decided fact that the time to be spent on oral work, will be different in different cases.

Current situation: These days, we find that teaching of reading is started on the first or second day of schooling. It is a great draw-back. There may be a number of reasons behind but it is cent percent a wrong step. So it is absolutely necessary that some times must be spent on aural-oral practice.

THE APPLICATION

Preparatory reading means preparing the students for reading from the books. When the students come to the school, they should not be taught reading on the first or the second day. Rather they should be given language training in listening, and speaking for some days. Thus oral work and its practice of one type or the other should continue for a number of days.

In preparatory stage, the teacher should teach the students how to produce certain sounds. They should be taught how to speak the words. Those words should be taken up in oral work which the students will conic across in their books at the later stage. This stage when the students are prepared for the stage of reading is also called pre-reading stage.

Thus we notice that preparatory reading is of utmost importance in the teaching of a language. The following steps are suggested for conducting it:

1. By showing actual objects, the teacher tells the names of the things. In case of verbs, actions are performed and the teacher speaks the words. The students simply watch and listen carefully.
2. The teacher makes use of charts or pictures for those items which cannot be actually shown by their sketches or diagrams can be drawn easily.
3. Flash cards can also be used for this purpose. On one flash card the name of the object is written and on the other, sketch is drawn. The teacher shows the flash cards and makes the students speak the words. By and by, he makes the picture disappear. It helps the students to have some recognition of the words or letters as the case may be.

4. In case the flash cards are not available, the blackboard can be used for the same purpose. Some of the pictures may be drawn and words or sentences describing them are written. Then the pupils are asked to read them, Later, only words or sentences may be written and pupils are helped to read them.
5. Some drills of words or sentences may be given in chorus, in groups and then to individuals.
6. By using blackboards or flash cards, simple comprehension drills may be conducted as mentioned below:
   (a) The learners may be asked to pick up one of the objects provided.
   (b) Some pictures may be provided, and the learner is asked to find one mentioned by the teacher.
   (c) First halves of a few sentences may be written on the blackboard. The second halves may be written on the flash cards. The students may be asked to pick- it the corresponding halves on the flash cards.
7. Some of the reading games may be introduced. These games are of two types:
   (i) Recognition games.
   (ii) Comprehension games.

Games for Recognition:

(a) Flash cards of some words in duplicate are prepared. One set is displayed on the board in front of the class and the second set is given to the students. The pupils are asked to match the words.

(b) Flash cards of some words in duplicate are prepared. Then the class is divided into two parts. One set of flash cards is distributed in one group and the other set is given to the students of the second group. Thus each student holds one flash card in his or her hand.

One student stands up and shows the flash card to the other group. The students of the other group read it out. Thus competition between the two groups is held. Of course, when the students have to speak the word, the time factor is controlled by the teacher.

Games for Comprehension:

The shop game: Each team is given a number of mixed flash cards containing the names of things to be found in three or four shops. The students sort them out properly shop-wise.

Read and do games: The teacher writes a number of sentences about actions on the blackboard and he numbers them. Thus he calls out the number of sentence and the name of a student. The student reads the sentence silently and does the action.

Teaching methods: Different methods of teaching reading have been popular from time to time. The methods even differ from country to country. Some of the popular methods are explained here below:

The alphabetic method: It is an old method of teaching reading. In this method, the students are taught the alphabets i.e. A, B, C- of the language. Here the unit of teaching is a letter. Later the students learn words by combining the alphabets.

It is a dull and boring method because the students are learning the alphabets A,B,C etc. which are meaningless. The small children do not feel interested in it. The teacher should try to make it interesting. *Walton* writes in his book. 'Principles and Methods of teaching'- "The Alphabetical Method insists upon a child attending separately to a dog's legs, tail etc. before allowing it to apprehend and name the animal as a whole " It is not a good method because it is lengthy and tedious. Moreover, there is too much emphasis on learning by rote.

The phonic method: It is a method of teaching reading in which each word is broken up into basic speech sounds. It really facilitates reading. Here the students are taught the different sounds first. They learn the alphabets afterwards. In other words, we can say that here the teacher teaches English through the phonetic script.

It is a very common method used in U.K. The only difficulty in its application is that there is need of expert teachers. That is one reason why this method did not become popular. In the words of *T.K.N. Menon* and *M.S. Patel*, "The Phonic Method was adopted when it was realized that the sounds of letters, not their names when uttered rapidly produce the word. It was also assumed that once these sounds had been learnt, they should be combined into syllables and words, then into larger language units. The method is most effective for languages in which the forms of letter invariably correspond with their sounds.

The word method: *P.C. Wren* calls it 'The One and Only Rational Method' of teaching to read. It is called Word Method because the unit of teaching is a word. Moreover, pictures are also used with the words. The students look at the picture and they say whatever they see. That is why, this method is also called 'Look and Say' method.

It is a very popular method of teaching reading. The learners remain motivated by this method. The only drawback in this method is that a good many pictures have to be used here. It is difficult to have pictures for some words such as a, the, to, of, from, at, etc. But this single drawback- remains nothing as compared to the good point of this method.

So we find that this method remains a distinguished method in comparison with other methods.

The Phrase Method: In this method, the unit of teaching is a phrase. The students learn phrases and they learn the alphabets afterwards. According to *Menon* and *Patel*, "The Phrase Method is based on the assumption that phrases are more interesting than words and place emphasis on meaning. It is believed that since good readers recognise group of words at each fixation of the eyes, the phrase method should foster rapid growth in efficient reading."

This method cannot be used for all types of children. The reason is that the weak- students can hardly pick up one word at a time. They find it hard to learn two or three words at a time.

The Sentence Method: In this method, the unit of teaching is a sentence. The students learn words and alphabets afterwards. This method cannot be used for all types of children. The reason is that average child cannot pick up one complete sentence at a time. This method can be used only in that case when the children are exceptionally good. *Schonel, Free I.* writes in his book, 'The Psychology and Teaching of Reading', "One of the greatest values of the sentence method lies in the help it offers to the pupil from the context and from the continuity that can be embodied in material."

Model Method: Out of the above mentioned methods of teaching reading, we find that none of them is perfect in every respect. So it is rather difficult to conclude that this method or that method is more useful and better than the other. Taken from the realities of class room situations point of view, we can say that we have to depend upon the combination of methods. So it is obvious that one and only one method cannot serve purpose in all types of situations and for all times to come. We have to be very careful while making the selection of a method for teaching purposes. Generally we make use of the -Word method' or 'Look and Say Method' which is a via media approach.

Thus by using the different methods, reading is taught to the students. At the initial stages, the learners may not be good readers but gradually the teacher is to enable them to read accurately and correctly by taking care of pauses.

Proper Eye-span: The teacher himself should present model reading to the learners by having proper eye movement. He should divide the sentence into phrases which are to be read together without any pause. Then he can give practice to the learners by setting time limit for reading any paragraph.

Defects and Remedies: While learning to read English, there may be many problems which the students will face. Some of the problems may be timely which will be solved automatically in due course of time. Thus at the initial stages, some of the letters which are slightly different in written representation may confuse the learners. For example, the letter m, n; c, e: It, k; y, z. This problem remains no problem when the learner will look at these letters again and again and be familiar with them. But there are some other problems which are not easy to tackle. This problem continually frightens the learners. Some students who are actively interested in the language, are able to get over those but others remain ill the grip of difficulty which may be a little bit or more. A few sounds of English which are different from the sounds of mother tongue may be misunderstood by the learners. For example/v/, /w/. They will produce both the sounds like Hindi sound. They will also confuse English sounds with Hindi and Punjabi sounds. Another problem in their way will be the problem of English spellings. English is not a phonetic language, but gradually they will tend to speak according to the written representation of the language. Then it will give rise to innumerable mistakes in reading. At the early stages, it is just possible that they may read the words in a funny way. For example, hat, and hut and shut and knife.

But these problems will not remain problems if sincere efforts are made to overcome all these difficulties. *A.W. Frisby* in his book 'English Teaching' has pointed out. There is no difficulty in teaching children to read. Many will teach themselves if we give them the right preparation, the right material and let them help each other. The young teacher should bear in mind that it is easier to teach pupils to read a new language than to speak it. At the same time, children should not be rushed into learning to read. The basis of sound reading method is that it presents in the form of signs material about which we have spoken and we must see that this principle is maintained. The material of reading follows the material of speech and when the pupil finds that he already knows that material and has only to learn to recognise the printed symbols for it, he will soon demonstrate his ability to read, to write labels for his pictures and attempt to read new. There must be ample language background before reading is attempted in earnest, and the richer the background is, the more easily will the pupils learn to read, apart from other considerations such as physical and intellectual equipment. Reading fits on the background of language experience. If this background is not there, learning to read will be a painful and frustrating experience of the pupil and the teacher. The background must be supplied by the agency of both home and school and will take the form of stories, discussions on pictures and a wide variety of conversation on ordinary experiences of life."

There are two types of learners who can be taught writing of English language. The first category is of those who have not learnt the writing of any language. The second category is of those who have already learnt the writing of mother tongue. In the first case, the teacher has to explain to the learners how they have to sit, how to hold a note book in the hand and how to hold a pen. After this, they are given preliminary practice of writing with a pen. Then they are given this type of practice with the help of chalks and small boards which are meant for the students. They are blackboards fixed up on the four walls.

Eleven

TEST OF ABILITY

The teaching learning process has been going on but its results have not been very effective. Tests and examinations have been conducted but very good results have not been seen. Evaluation which is a broader term than tests and examinations is expected to serve the purposes better.

English language teaching needs better application of evaluation. That is likely to improve the teaching learning process.

In evaluation, the work of the students is assessed continuously. All round assessment of the learners is made throughout the year. It involves objectives of teaching, methods to achieve them and then finding out how far they have been achieved. The ultimate objectives of language teaching are comprehension and expression.

The four skills of language learning i.e. listening, speaking, reading and writing ultimately achieve these objectives. Evaluation certainly aims at improving the abilities in the acquisition of four skills.

VARIOUS ASPECTS

To make the programme of continuous and comprehensive evaluation a success, unit approach in teaching and testing will hold good. The whole of the syllabus which is to be covered in the whole of the year is divided into some units. Each unit consists of material which is almost of similar type. The total duration of the academic session is also divided into some parts-say a unit of syllabus for every month or for two weeks or three weeks.

Thus teaching is done for the syllabus given in the unit and after covering that much of the syllabus, test is given to the learners out of the syllabus marked for that unit. This type of approach is called unit approach.

Unlike traditional testing at the end of the year, unit teaching and unit testing make the instructional work more meaningful. The teacher is able to do justice to his duty of teaching. The learners are also able to prepare well. This approach does not allow the teacher or the students to skip over certain portions of the syllabus.

Unit approach is bound to make the continuous and comprehensive programme of evaluation of success.

IDEAL PLAN

Here below are suggested a few steps which will help in making evaluation all successful:

1. Continuous comprehensive evaluation can be made successful if UNIT APPROACH is adopted in teaching and testing. In unit approach, a block of closely related subject matter is taught and thereafter a test is given to the students. It gives continuous feed-back to both the teacher and the taught. So they can improve accordingly.
2. Head of the institutions and the teaching staff should

be trained for the purpose of internal evaluation. This job may be entrusted to DIETS set up in different districts. The DIETS should work in collaboration with teacher training colleges, SCERT and N.C.E.R.T.

3. Different criteria may be fixed up for different items. Accordingly assessment of the learners should be made.
4. In each institution, moderation committees be set up with the Head of the Institution as its chairman. Thus all assessment should be subject to the review of moderation committee.
5. Tuition work on the part of the teachers should be banned completely.
6. Any type of evil if spreads anywhere in the institutions, be taken up seriously with strict action against the defaulter. The policy should be to nip the evil in the bud.

Merits

(1) Every teacher knows well about his students. Whatever may be the subject or area of study, only the teacher.

DIFFERENT GROWTH MODELS

Though education, the social aspect of an individual is developed. The teacher is expected to test the sociability of every pupil. It can be done in the following ways:

1. The teacher takes into consideration the work being done by a student daily, his participation in games, social service, cleanliness etc.
2. Proficiency in various co-curricular activities should be seen. For this a five point scale may be prepared. A variety of opportunities may be provided to the students in which they may freely display their qualities like sociability, cooperation, sympathetic attitude, self-help etc.

Education helps in the development of good health and right habits. The pupil is able to develop himself physically. It is the duty of the teacher that he should assess the physical development of the pupils from time to time. He should try to diagnose the disabilities.

Physical handicaps etc. with the assistance of school doctor and help in the immediate cure programme for assessing the physical development will be as under:

(1) A doctor should be engaged in the school for part time or full time duty.

(2) Arrangements be made for physico-medical test after every 3 or 4 months.

(3) A record of medical check-up should be kept. Remedial measures accordingly should be used.

(4) Students' participation in games and athletics should be recorded.

(5) Physical efficiency of each pupil should be measured by using a rating scale.

THE ASSIMILATION-ORIENTED TEST

External examinations, as a technique of evaluation, have failed to meet the desired ends. Let us see how far the technique of continuous comprehensive evaluation will be useful.

Evaluation is continuous and comprehensive. When we have it fully internal without the help of the external agencies, it is called Internal Evaluation. In that case, the teachers preparing the students in the class rooms are to judge fully and finally the performance of their own students. All types of achievements of the students, scholastic and non-scholastic are evaluated continuously for the whole session. The whole record of the student is maintained properly in the cumulative record register and on that basis, pass or fail of a students is determined by the teaching personnels of the school.

Continuous comprehensive internal evaluation is different from internal assessment. In case of internal assessment, external examination and its fears hang like a sword in the minds of the learners as well as the teachers. Internal assessment is just a part of external examination. Some people might argue that in internal assessment, our educational institutions have no good experiences and that way internal evaluation may not prove a farce. Continuous comprehensive internal evaluation seems to be the panacea of all the ills that are being faced through the process of traditional examinations. It is high time that we make evaluation an integral part of the total teaching learning process.

That way our testing will become comprehensive as it will take care of all the three domains for all-around development of the learner in both the scholastic and the non-scholastic areas. The current system of giving divisions in the examinations and thus classifying the learners into classes should be ousted. It should give place to unit tests which should be administered regularly to judge over all personality of the child in the light of objectives fixed up.

GOAL-ORIENTED TEST

Objectives of teaching English are framed in the light of over all environment of the child which includes social, political, national, cultural and economic aspects of life. Those objectives naturally include scholastic and non-scholastic areas. Through continuous evaluation judgement about the child is made continuously. The objective and the efforts to achieve those objectives remain in the process of review and revision till the desired ends are achieved.

Communication: Evaluation is comprehensive in the sense that the over all personality of the child is assessed. In all spheres of life, learner's acquisition of four skills of language i.e. listening, speaking, reading and writing are taken care of in evaluation.

Continual Process: Continuous evaluation helps the teachers in knowing about their effects side by side and so they improve accordingly. The learners also come to know their deficiency with regard to different things and thus they can remedy the same by taking proper guidance and making more efforts.

The Requirement: The need of the times is to make evaluation an integral part of the total teaching learning process. Testing should also be comprehensive so that all the three domains for all round development of the learner in both the scholastic and the non-scholastic areas are fully covered. Unlike the traditional system of testing which takes into consideration only the academic side, evaluation aims at testing all the aspects of the personality of the learners.

CLASSICAL GOAL-ORIENTED TEST

In order to evaluate the scholastic achievement of a student, the following tools which supplement each other will be used:

Written Examination: Written examination includes questions of essay type, short answer type and objective type.

(i) *Essay Type Tests* have law validity and reliability but still we cannot dispense with them. We need them for measuring the essential skills such as application of knowledge, solution of problems, expression etc.

(ii) *Short Answer Type Tests* have more validity and reliability as compared to essay type. So those will be used.

(iii) *Objective Type or New Type Tests* are still more reliable. They are comprehensive, easy to score and less time consuming. By using these we ran measure the ability to organise knowledge, express things and narrate facts.

All the three i.e. essay type, short answer type and objective type tests supplement each other.

Oral Test: These are used for testing skills which are not tested by written tests, for example, pronunciation, speed and accuracy of reading a book, comprehension and verbal expression, reciting a poem, answering questions orally etc. All these are possible through oral tests. Formal tests, interview, observation may also be used.

Sessionals Evaluated: Sessional work done by a student is also important. Apart from written and oral examinations, sessional work is also to be assessed.

Assessment of sessional work includes the following:

(a) Home assignment done by the student.

(b) Impression of the teacher formed on the basis of class discussions etc.

(c) Use of library.

(d) Practical work done in language laboratory.

Personality Evaluated: Education helps in the over-all development of a person. So the different traits of personality and character of an individual should be assessed. The different traits are expressed by an individual in day to day's behaviour. The teacher should record the behaviour of a student inside the class room and outside the class room, in the library, in the laboratory, in the playground, in the field of other activities etc. It can be better done in the following ways:

1. The pupil's diary which he himself maintains should be assessed.
2. Assessment of the diary maintained by the teacher for recording the behaviour of the students be made.
3. Personality test may be given from time to time.

Twelve

BEYOND TEACHING AND LEARNING

For the purpose of harmonious development of the child personality, it is inevitable not only to expose him to scholastic areas for intellectual development but also to put him in situations where he may get opportunities to work with his hands and develop proper attitudes towards manual labour. In addition, there is an urgent need to bridge the gap between the world of school and the world of work.

This gap will widen further, if not controlled, due to the modern technological developments and the increasingly technology-based society of the future. Processes and skills of work are changing. An clearly initiation of children into these is possible only through work experience or socially useful productive work (SUPW).

That is why the Education Commission (1964-66) made a strong case for introducing work experience as an essential component of general education at all stages of school education. As a matter of fact, the work experience or SUPW approach should permeate the entire curriculum.

SUPW provides the basis for the development of knowledge, skills and attitudes useful for latter participation in productive work. SUPW should cover production, maintenance and the technological process as well as human relations, organisation and management and marketing. The areas of work chosen should have local significance and should be such as to develop the competence of the students. It is not just learning to work, it is work education.

SUPW programmes can serve the following objectives. Their main purpose should be to develop proper attitudes towards work, to inculcate dignity of labour, banish status and class distinctions, and to stress the principle of productivity. Whenever possible SUPW should help to appreciate the need for and utility of labour-saving devices, gadgets, tools that are so much a part of modern life, and the techniques involved in their use and the underlying scientific principles.

Various activities of SUPW must necessarily be related to the community needs and its services. A carefully directed SUPW programme would also help to discover the aptitude of a student for gainful vocations which demand certain types of skills, physical ability, attitudes towards others with whom they have to work and responsibility in performing their Jobs and discharging their duties.

At the primary stage, SUPW should begin with simple, creative, self-expressional activities performed with locally available material and simple tools. It is desirable to avoid any activity with an element of monotony in it. At middle and secondary levels, the use of the tools should be introduced in a scientific manner.

As a science teacher you are likely to teach also some SUPW subject along with science subjects — Physics, Chemistry and Biology. It is a general practice in schools that physics teachers teach electronics and electrical gadgets, chemistry teachers teach photography, and biology teachers teach gardening. It is not necessary that science teachers should only teach some science based SUPW subject. They may also develop and teach SUPW Course selecting some activities according to .their interest from the list given in the suggested SUPW syllabus given in this chapter or adding some other activities from their own experiences. Some activities like cleanliness suggested in the syllabus may be useful and interesting in any subject as well as in science.

If you learn, therefore, to teach some SUPW subjects in your B.Ed. programme you may be an asset to the school where you will teach science as a regular teacher, otherwise you will need an immediate in-service teacher training to teach SUPW course, as soon as you join a school as a regular teacher.

PLAN FOR LITERACY

Before discussing any enrichment programme it will be desirable to describe the students for whom these programmes are needed — enrichment programmes are needed for gifted children to fulfil their demands.

I. The gifted children have been defined in many ways. One acceptable version in gifted are those who by virtue of outstanding abilities are capable of high performance and are identified by professionally qualified persons. They include all the following:

   (a) *Talented:* Those students who may be talented in one or few fields.

   (b) *Intelligent:* Students who score high on intelligent test (verbal or non-verbal), they may be with an IQ of 130 or above.

   (c) *Creative:* Creative children are intelligent, talented plus they have something extra; they are also productive thinkers.

   (d) *Skilled:* They are capable of performing better in psychomotor abilities.

II. The gifted children can be identified by some of their behavioural characteristics as described by T. Renzulli and R. Hartman in their scale for rating behavioural characteristics of superior Students.

A. In their *Learning* characteristics, they:

(i) usually have advanced vocabulary for their age and grade level.

(ii) are keen and alert observers, usually see more to get a more out of a description and films etc.

(iii) read great deal on their own, prefer adult level books.

B. Regarding *Motivational* characteristics, they:

(iv) get easily bored with routine task.

(v) are not easily satisfied with their own speed or products.

(vi) often pass judgement or events, people and things.

C. In their *Creative* characteristics, they:

(vii) display great deal of curiosity, ask questions.

(viii) display a good deal of intellectual playfulness, manipulate ideas *i.e.,* change and elaborate upon them.

D. About their *Leadership* characteristics, they:

(ix) are self-confident with children of their own age as well as adults.

(x) adapt readily to new situations, are flexible in thoughts and actions.

Some enrichment programmes which are used to fulfil the demands of gifted are described here.

Acceleration: It means skipping classes, it may be in one subject or more subjects or by some other means shortening the time spent on studies.

Special Grouping: Here the opportunity is given for special education in each homogenous group based on abilities.

Enrichment Programmes: Special academic provision for various students.

One technique used to cope up with the gifted student is accelerating the phase by skipping classes. This technique benefits the individual without changing the actual educational programme. For many years, most of the people, educators and administrators have understood the word acceleration only in terms of skipping ' class or classes. But it has shown results that skipping classes is least desirable method of acceleration. Many emotional, psychological problems may arise in some children when they are not able to adjust in the new peer group.

In United States of America some other methods of acceleration are being used successfully. Some such methods are, early admission to primary school, i.e. before the normal age of 6 years, upgraded primary and middle schools, students are allowed to move up for one or two subjects for example a 6th grade child is doing 7th or 8th grade maths or science, students are allowed to take extra load in terms of extra credits in senior classes to be able to finish school early to get early admission in College. The advanced placement programme has become a popular method of stimulating high aptitude students in high schools.

Acceleration does not necessarily work for each gifted child. A thorough knowledge of needs and abilities of the individual is required to accomplish success with minimum personal problems.

Some results of the research studies on acceleration are described here to get a better understanding.

Terman and Odem (1947) suggested as a result of their follow-up study.

It is our opinion that nearly all children of 135 IQ or higher should be promoted sufficiently to permit college entrance by the age of 17 at least, and majority of this group would be better if entering at 16. Acceleration of this extent is especially desirable for those who plan to complete two or more years of graduate study in preparation for a professional career.

Callagher (1966), in summarising research on the topic reported:

> "The recent research on acceleration has done nothing to change the generally favourable portrait of these methods for moderately shortening the educational career of talented youth. The advantage of saving a year or two from a long investment in educational time does not seem diluted by social or emotional difficulties."

Reynolds, Brich and Tuseth (1962), in reviewing research on evaluation of early admittance programmes, commented as follows:

> "It may be concluded, from the research that early admission to school of mentally advanced children who were within a year of the ordinary school entrance age and who are generally mature is to their advantage. There are few issues in education on which the research evidence now available is so clear and so universally favourable to a particular solution."

As far as we are concerned in India with the present system of education there is not much scope of acceleration except a little early admission to primary classes.

COLLABORATIVE PLAN

Another way of solving this problem is the grouping of students according to their abilities. One of the questions often asked in educational circles is "what is the impact of ability grouping." One of the most comprehensive studies was carried by Goldberg, Passion Just Man and Hagg (1965). The author concluded that merely changing the ability grouping within the class without changing the curriculum or the manner in which the children were taught could not be expected to produce any substantial changes.

Goldberg has commented: "Ability grouping is by no means a sufficient condition ensuring greater academic achievement at any ability level. At best, it provides a framework within which enhanced learning may be more effectively planned and executed." Hence to solve the problem of gifted (as well as backward) the ability grouping should be subject-wise with differentiated curricula. For example, in physics, chemistry, biology, maths, there should be at least three types of courses, one for more able in that subject, other for average and the third for below average or the slow learners.

The subject to subject ability grouping in different subjects is only possible if the timetable is made student-wise not section-wise, because a student in higher ability group in one subject may not necessarily be fit for higher ability groups in all the subjects. In American schools the students move from class to class and the subject rooms are fixed.

Such homogeneous ability groups are made, and different courses in each subject are being taught, for example, higher ability students are offering BSCS Blue version and low ability students are doing "Pattern and Processes" or some such similar courses of various abilities.

In our country in some schools sections are made according to the ability of the students and also some courses were being offered at various levels. A (higher) and B (lower) level courses in science (physics, chemistry, biology) were being offered in various sections from 1979 at secondary level. The more able students in science were able to offer A-level courses and uninterested and uninvolved average students were able to take B-level courses. Now the Central Board of Secondary Education, New Delhi has proposed again a common course for all from 1984.

There are advantages and disadvantages of this homogeneous grouping. On one hand in ability grouping the teaching can be modified according to the need of the students in a more effective way but on the other hand they get labelled as A and B grade students.

In Delhi, the New Delhi Municipal Council (NDMC) has started several separate schools for talented students called Nav Yug Schools. Here the admissions are given to only gifted children after some testing. But the courses are the same as in other schools.

ACQUIRING KNOWLEDGE

Enrichment can be defined as the type of activity devoted to the further development of the particular intellectual skills and talents of the gifted child.

For many years more conscious teachers are using the technique of enrichment for fulfilling the need of gifted child. "Rich" means physical accumulation and "enrich" means richness at the mental level. The question is how should we specially as a science teacher enrich the gifted students so that they will be properly groomed for future.

For any kind of enrichment programmes following preliminaries are important:

(i) Identification and listing of gifted students in your class or classes.

(ii) Identification of modifications or enrichment techniques to be given to bright individuals.

Gifted and talented students when exposed, always accept the challenging situations and if guided properly give very encouraging results. There are some qualities which are found in gifted students, these should be developed to a maximum potential. Some of these qualities are:

- reasoning through complex problems
- abstract thinking
- originality in views and effort
- association and interrelation of concepts
- giving generalisations
- drawing relationships
- curiosity to learn and read
- create new ideas and originate new lines of thought
- have wider interests.

Some or all of these qualities are present to some extent in gifted children but a proper environment is required for their development The task is not easy for most teachers but as a science teacher one should try to take the challenge for helping the students and the society.

Broadly speaking there can be two types of enrichment programmes.

Horizontal, Breadth or Lateral Enrichment Programmes: In this type of programme enrichment can be given in relating the topic with other related topics. For example, while teaching photosynthesis relation to stoma to and other related metabolic activities can be taken as enrichment.

Vertical, Depth or Intensive Enrichment Programmes: In such cases gifted students can be given more intensive, detailed or in depth study of the topic. For example, Kreb Cycle is taught in a simple way upto X class, the gifted students can be given details of the biochemistry to learn the concept more effectively.

To keep these two aspects in mind the different assignments can be planned for various ability students in a normal classroom. Some teachers in their effort of giving some kind of enrichment programme to the gifted give longer and more extensive assignments of the usual sort. This kind of assignment is not fulfilling the need of the gifted.

Some talented students may get disinterested with such assignments. Here the opportunity should be given to explore and do things on their own rather than giving the assignment of the same intellectual level.

In a normal classroom situation this is the least a teacher can do to help gifted as well as backward to give variations in assignments according to their needs. While planning your lesson you should also plan varied assignments for different students. The assignments can be given as options without obvious description of gifted and backward etc.

Although the teachers were always free to plan and give enrichment programmes in the form of special assignments and extra readings etc., this kind of provision was not given in the traditional science curricula.

SCHEMES FOR SLOW LEARNERS

There are children in science classes who are not motivated to learn science. They are slow in learning than average students, they are weak intellectually and emotionally. They are also called backward children.

Backward Children: Backward children are those having I.Q. below average, usually they are slow in learning. In our normal schools we are mostly concerned with border-line cases.

An acceptable educational defination of backward child is one who is not able to do the work of one year below. If a VI class child is not able to do V class work he can be considered as backward.

It is also possible that a student is considered backward in one subject and not in others.

The enthusiasm of slow learners tend to be short-lived.

Apart from a limited attention span within a lesson, there is a strict limit to the length of the time that a teacher can spend on any topic before it loses appeal.

It is easier to teach those who want to learn science than it is to teach those who do not. This will be a challenge to teach science to slow learners. This challenge should be taken by science teachers not as a burden but with pleasure.

I. D.S. Robertson of Jordentiff College Education Glasgow has listed some skills and qualities to be developed in slow learners. They are as follows:

(i) The ability to communicate in speech and writing and to read with understanding.

(ii) The ability to make measurement and do calculations.

(iii) Capacities for thought, judgement, discrimination and enjoyment.

(iv) Responsibility for their work.

(v) An understanding of the physical world and the society in which they live.

(vi) A vocabulary for discussion of current events and issues in science.

(vii) An appreciation of the importance of personal relationship and the value of cooperative effect.

(viii) An ability to find out scientific information for themselves.

(ix) An awareness of the variety of ways in which leisure time can be used.

(x) Self-confidence, self-respect, and as realistic an idea of one's own capabilities and potential as is possible.

Virtually all these qualities can be fostered within the teaching of science, and it is thus important that one should think of education through teaching rather than of teaching science as an end in itself.

The same objectives could well be achieved through a study of different topics in science. When choosing science content to meet these objectives, the following questions should be kept in mind by the teacher.

(i) Is the material relevant? In other words, will the pupils see the material as useful to them either at the time they are in school, or after they have left school.

(ii) Is the material capable of being presented in an interesting way?

(iii) Is the material within the pupils' powers of comprehension.

Remedial Programme: Special programmes are needed for above average and below average students both to cope up with their needs.

Special Grouping: As discussed in the case of gifted special grouping according to the abilities of slow learner has been identified as an effective way, if special curricula are also given to them. Even if special programmes for slow learners are not available, at least the teacher can develop a teaching style which will be more effective for slow learners.

Many special curricula in sciences have been developed in USA and United Kingdom where stress is on experimentation and the materials are tailored to their unique characteristics and needs. The content covered is comparatively less, and more real experiences are given. Science is studied in its social context including problems of society related to various science subjects.

BSCS has developed a special curricula for below average students "pattern and processes".

Another programme developed for educationally uninvolved students is "Ideas and Investigation in Science" (Biology and Physical Science).

In our country we do not have special ability grouping and

special curricula for slow learners in regular schools. The A and B level science courses (CBSE) discussed above are for above average and average students respectively, and there are no special courses for slow learners, and even these two courses merged in 1984.

Remedial Programmes: Like enrichment programmes for gifted students some remedial programmes are also designed for slow learners. Programme instruction works very well with slow learners because of self-pacing. Therefore, special curricula developed for slow learners also include simple programmed materials.

In most of the Indian schools there is provision for a remedial period in the beginning or at the end of the school hours. Very few teachers are using this period for actual remedial work.

Many a times teachers use this period to cover the course or to revise the course in a full class. This period should be utilised only for actual remedial work for the few students who have been identified as slow learners and actually need teacher's help.

Role of the Teacher: The teacher has to be patient with slow learners, they need care and love. They develop hatred if they are not properly cared as they are emotionally weak.

Students can learn more if the teacher makes the learning "Child Centred" as far as possible. The students should be allowed to become active agents in the educational process.

A warm but firm hand, and a real concern is required for slow learners. The teacher should praise the slow learners frequently. The teacher should help the students to achieve success. This will encourage them to work hard, and they will devote more time in studies. Thus they will be able to learn just about the same devoting more time what average students learn in less time.

MAIN OBJECTIVES

The objectives of SUPW may be stated as follows:

(i) To prepare students to practise and perform manual work individually and collectively;

(ii) To acquaint students with the world of work and services to the community and develop in them a sense of respect for manual work;

(iii) To develop a desire to be useful members of society and contribute their best to the common good;

(iv) To indicate positive attitudes of team work and socially desirable values like self-reliance, dignity of labour, tolerance, cooperation, sympathy and helpfulness;

(v) To help in understanding the principles involved in the various forms of work;

(vi) To lead children to participate increasingly in productive work as they go from one stage of education to another and, thereby, enable them to earn while they learn;

(vii) To provide opportunities of creative self-expression and for the development of problem solving abilities;

(viii) To provide for the development of vocational preparedness;

(ix) To develop in the students an awareness of social problems and inculcate in them positive attitudes towards community service.

GAINFUL WORK

The SUPW syllabus should be flexible. It is not desirable to prescribe a uniform SUPW syllabus for all the schools, as is the practice with other subjects. The SUPW syllabus should depend upon the local needs and facilities available. It is suggested that SUPW syllabus should have three components:

(i) Study of the world of work through observation and enquiry;

(ii) Experimentation with material, tools and techniques; and

(iii) Work practice.

The first two components are concerned with preparation for actual participation in productive work and services. This makes the common core programme of SUPW. The third component, "work practice" may lead to remuneration or earning. Thus the SUPW syllabus will have two components:

(a) A common core programme, comprising components (i) and (ii) above, and

(b) Work practice, the third component of the syllabus.

The purpose of the common core programme will be to bring about attitudinal changes and to develop readiness for work practice. The purpose of work practice is to give a vocational bias to the programme. It will, therefore, be repetitive in nature and, it is hoped that it will be remunerative either in kind or cash. When framing SUPW syllabus, the content identified may be put in the following six areas:

(i) Health and Hygiene;

(ii) Food;

(iii) Shelter;

(iv) Clothing;

(v) Culture and Recreation; and

(vi) Community Work and Social Service.

Some suggestive activities for various levels pertaining to the above six areas are as follows.

SPECIAL PROFIT

Common Core Programme

(i) *Health and Hygiene:* Dusting of furniture, cleaning of classrooms and science laboratories, school buildings, the school compound and its vicinity.

(ii) *Food:* Vegetable gardening or pot culture, cooking of meals.

(iii) *Shelter:* Construction with plastic, pliable and rigid material, maintenance of articles of use.

(iv) *Clothing:* Spinning and simple hand weaving or knitting, washing of clothes, stitching, mending.

(v) *Culture and Recreation:* Recreating the classroom, preparation for important national days, festivals and school function.

(vi) *Community Work and Social Service:* Cleaning the neighbourhood, planting and care of shade trees, running of cooperative stores, the school panchayat, helping adults in productive work.

Work Practice: This should be in the form of projects. A suggestive list is as follows: Few projects according to the need and interest of students and availability of time may be selected in each class from the following list.

(i) *Health and Hygiene:* Making of tooth powder, soap, disinfectants, detergent powder, hair oil, brooms, waste paper baskets, dust bins, first-aid boxes, health posters, scrap books on health and hygiene, keeping health records, keeping the neighbourhood clean, working at health centres.

(ii) *Food:* Growing of selected vegetables and flower plants in plots or pots — where possible, also for sale; seed collecting, soil testing, experimentation with different kinds of soils, different types of seeds, different kinds of manures; vegetative propagating, by grafting of propagation by breeding, vegetative propagation by grafting, vegetative reproductivity, layering, soil conservation; making of jam, jelly, ketchup, sauce, pickles, fruit juices, confectionery or bakery items; working in canteen, or stalls for a specified period; packing of food material.

(iii) *Shelter:* Making stationery items, white washing, polishing doors, windows and furniture; caning chairs, repairs of furniture, casual labour work in the school.

(iv) *Clothing:* Spinning, making school bags, school uniforms, handkerchiefs, table cloths, pillow cases, knitting, making mats.

(v) *Culture and Recreation:* Toy making, artificial flowers making, pottery painting, making games material, greeting cards, fancy covers for book and book binding, fancy candle making.

(vi) *Community Work and Social Service:* Helping adults in their work as projects, such as keeping a specified area clean, helping in the case of the sick, first-aid, helping at functions and during festivals, traffic control, helping in the literacy campaign.

At this level more emphasis should be given to work practice. A suggestive list of activities (crafts/services) is given below, some activities according to the need and interest of students and availability of time may be selected in each class from the following list.

(i) *Health and Hygiene:* Growing medicinal plants, eradication of communicable diseases, paramedical service; cleanliness of the neighbourhood, well and pond, and die disposal of garbage; construction of toilet facilities and composite pits; making tooth picks, tooth powder, soap, detergents, disinfectants, first-aid boxes; construction of waste-paper baskets, dust bins, garbage cans, brooms, brushes, dusters, mops etc.; detection of adulteration.

(ii) *Food:* Agro-industries; kitchen gardening; pot culture; crop and seed production; repair of farm implements; soil conservation and desert control; horticulture, animal husbandry, and dairying, beekeeping, poultry farming, fish culture, distribution of fertilisers and insecticides, processing and preservation of food, hydroponics, mushroom culture; khandsari, gur and candy making; canning; making jam, jelly, squashes, pickles; packing food, marketing, bakery; confectionary, cooking.

(iii) *Shelter:* Pottery, masonry work, workshop practice — mechanical, electrical, electronics; cane and bamboo work; black-smithy, wood work, carpet weaving; home, village and town planning; minor repairs in buildings, fittings, furniture and household articles, decorating the home, gardening, interior decorations, construction of decorative pieces, chalk and candle making.

(iv) *Clothing:* Production of cotton, wool, silk and other fibres, weaving, dress making, knitting, hosiery work, embroidery work, dress designing, leather work, spinning of different fibres; dyeing, printing and repair of garments, laundry work.

(v) *Culture and Recreation:* Making toys and puppets, making and repairing musical instruments; making games material, printing, book binding, photography, stage craft, making costumes, holding exhibitions.

(vi) *Community Work and Social Service:* Identification of problems relating to health and hygiene, supply of drinking water and adult literacy; rendering help in solving these problems; helping teachers in tackling school drop-out problem by visiting houses of children and finding out their difficulties; motivating the people in slum and unhygienic areas to maintain cleanliness of their surroundings by joining hands with them in cleanliness campaigns; helping the illiterate people in the community by way of writing letters, filling in application forms and reading telegrams for them; helping in road construction and digging of well etc. in the community and their maintenance; during natural calamities involving students in the relief work and help the people in the affected areas; serving the sick people in the community; tree plantation; checking the soil erosion; canal repair and maintenance.

(a) *Common Core Programme:* The work done in the previous classes should be further extended at this level.

(b) *Work Practice:* This should include mass production of work done previously as well as community and social work.

(c) *Subject Related Suggested SUPW Activities*

Physics: Gaining the basic knowledge about how to prevent electric shock accidents; giving the knowledge about how the lightning and the thunder occur and what are the use of lightning and thunder; giving an idea about how we receive the sound from the radio which is relayed from the radio station: preparing hot water with the help of solar heat energy; giving the knowledge about how to produce artificial rain; giving an idea of how to get electricity from the water and the steam; giving the basic knowledge about how to operate the machines like washing machine, grinding machine, electric cookers etc.; giving the knowledge about how the sound is produced from various sound instruments; giving them the basic knowledge and practice about electronics and electrical gadgets.

Chemistry: Preparation of soap and washing soda; explaining the uses of dettol and phenyl for cleanliness: preparation of tincture-iodine and .simple ointments for wounds; preparation of dyes; explaining the preparation of bleaching powder; explaining the equipping technique and uses of gobar gas plant in the houses making use of animal waste; explaining the uses and preparation of ammonium nitrate; explaining the fixation of nitrogen; explaining the uses of insecticides; demonstrating the method of purifying water;

giving them the basic knowledge and practice about various processes involved in photography.

Biology: Helping the farmers to get rid of the insect pest; learning methods of vegetative propagation; introducing modern techniques of incubation in poultry; practising the way of getting uniform fruiting and blossoming through simple techniques using chemicals (hormones); leathering of economically important animals; making them aware of economic zoology; providing them the knowledge of crop rotation; helping them to know about the various sources of nitrogen manure in the form of nitrogen yielding plants (legumes) and easily available cultures to increase the yield; making them aware of contamination; giving them the basic knowledge and practice about various processes and techniques involved in gardening.

THE EVALUATION

The evaluation work in SUPW should be carried out at three levels:

(i) By the teacher;

(ii) By the children; and

(iii) By the parents and community members.

The teacher should note the behaviour of children and the skills learnt by them during SUPW activities. The students should maintain diary of the daily work and experiences gained along with their reactions. The parents and the community members involved in organising SUPW activities should be consulted while assessing students behaviour and participation.

(i) *Attendance:* A record of attendance should be maintained in SUPW classes (indoor or outdoor) as is usually done in other subject classes.

(ii) *Observation:* What needs to be evaluated is not only the product (goods or services), but also the process and the quality of learning, for which observation is a reliable technique. 'Anecdotal Records' and 'Check lists' may be used when this techniques of evaluation is used.

(iii) *Self-evaluation:* Self-evaluation of their work by the students may prove to be a good measure. It may lead to some exaggerations in the beginning but, if persisted in, will turn out to be a very reliable tool of evaluation.

(iv) *Written Tests:* Written examination in SUPW does not seem to be necessary. It may cause even some disadvantages. Assessment, therefore, should take the form of *demonstration, viva voce, or examination of the product or service.*

(v) *Feedback from Parents:* Parents and guardians may be able to give valuable feedback of their children's work (SUPW) at home, which will help the teacher in evaluation.

(vi) *Feedback from Community Members:* In case of community service projects, the assessment by the beneficiaries may also be a good source of evaluation.

According to the Central Board of Education (CBSE), New Delhi, the assessment should be done on the following 7 points scale:

Grade A (Excellent)	75 percent and above
Grade B (Very Good)	60-74 percent
Grade C (Good)	53-59 percent
Grade D (Quite Satisfactory)	45-52 percent
Grade E (Just Satisfactory)	33-44 percent
Grade F (Poor)	15-32 percent
Grade G (Very Poor) Below	15 percent

In order to ensure that the objectives of SUPW programme are achieved, it is necessary to follow the problem solving approach. Students should be made aware of the problems related to their needs; they should be led to arrive at solutions by discussing the material, tools and techniques necessary for performing such work and services. A built-in system of evaluation should be developed to enable the students to improve their performance and to enable teachers to give a fair assessment of their work.

IMPROVEMENT AND SOLUTION METHOD

There are children not of different ages but also of different abilities in the same class. There are children who are from different socio-economic backgrounds, who have different values and different outlook.

There are children who require differentiated educational programme and services beyond those normally provided by the regular school programmes. These programmes can be enrichment programmes and remedial programmes.

MEANING AND HISTORY

The concept of manual work as a tool of education is not very new in our country. It was recognised long before the advent of formal education. In ancient India the students used to live in their schools *(ashrams)* with their teacher *(guru)*. They had to do every kind of manual work for living and learning. Education was related to the life of students and the dichotomy between education and work was not existing.

When formal education was introduced in the country, education became bookish and it started preparing students for white collared jobs. There was no provision of manual work in formal education. This limitation was pointed out in the Woods Education Despatch (1854) which contemplated the introduction of pre-vocational education at the secondary stage. But practically, no action was taken in this direction. Wood and Abbott (1937) also stressed the need of manual work in education for the sake of harmonious development of child's personality.

Deploring the ineffectiveness of bookish education, Rabindra Nath Tagore also stressed the role of manual work in education for all-round development of the child. Mahatma Gandhi insisted for the first time that education should centre around manual and productive work. This proposal of Mahatma Gandhi was accepted at the Wardha National Education Conference in October 1937.

This proposal when accepted was given a practical shape by the Zakir Hussain Committee and Basic Education was accepted as the national pattern of education at the primary level in 1938.

Kothari Commission (1966) suggested that Work Experience should form an integral part of general education (Class I to X). The Commission also clarified that the concept of work-experience was essentially similar to the Mahatma Gandhi's philosophy of Basic Education and it might be described as a redefinition of his thinking in terms of the changes in society due to the development of industrialisation. Consequently, great emphasis was given to work experience in the new 10+2 pattern of education.

In June 1977, Ishwarbhai Patel Committee pointed out that "work-experience which was intended to be an integral feature of the curriculum, at all stages, did not find a proper place in teaching-learning process that followed the introduction of the new pattern." This Committee recommended a scheme having three components — humanities, science, and work (Socially Useful Productive Work and Community Services), together with aesthetic appreciation to illuminate the curriculum.

Adiseshiah Committee also accepted the concept and objectives of Socially Useful Productive Work (SUPW) as defined by Ishwarbhai Patel Committee, for plus two stage with minor modifications.

The National Education Conference (December 18 to 20,1977) held in New Delhi, under the chairmanship of Shri Sriman Narain, recommended that 50 per cent of the total school time ought to be devoted to productive, creative and recreational activities, at least half of which should be focused on SUPW of various kinds. It also urged, as did Patel Committee, that the existing burden on student of textbooks, due to a large number of compulsory subjects, should be tided proportionately.

BIBLIOGRAPHY

Aggarwal, J.C.: *Development and Planning of Modern Education with Special Reference to India,* Vikas Publishing House, New Delhi, 1982.

Andrew W. Halping: *Administrative Theory in Education,* The MacMillan Company, New York, 1967.

Bansal, R.K.: *Introduction to English Teaching, Phonetics and Spoken English,* CIEFL, OUP, Hyderabad, 1990.

Bansal, R.K. and Harrison, J.B.: *Spoken English for India,* Orient Longman, New Delhi, 1983.

Bhatia, K.K.: *New Techniques of Teaching English as a Foreign Language,* NBS Educational Publishers, Chandigarh, 1988.

Desai, A.R.: *Papers in the Sociology of Education in India,* NCERT, New Delhi, 1990.

Frisby, A.W.: *Teaching English: Notes and Comments in Teaching English Overseas,* ELBS, London, 1970.

Gaur, J.S. and Saraswat, R.K.: *Occupational Literature: An Annotated Bibliography,* NCERT, New Delhi, 1978.

Gupta, P.K.: *Teaching of English,* R. Lall Book Depot, Meerut, 2001.

Haragopal, G.: *Administrative Leadership and Rural Development in India,* Light & Life Publishers, New Delhi, 1980.

John W., Hanson and Cole S. Brem Beck: *Education and the Development of Nations*, Holt, Rinehart and Winston, New York, 1966.

Kohli, A.L.: *Teaching of English*, Dhanpat Rai and Sons, Jallandhar, 2003.

Louis Malassis: *The Rural World: Education and Development*, Croom Helm, London, 1976.

Mukherji, S.N.: *Administration of Education in India*, Acharya Book Depot, Baroda, 1962.

Niblett, W.R.: *Essential Education*, University of London, London,1955.

Prem Kripal: *A Decade of Education in India*, Indian Book Company, Delhi, 1968.

Rudolph & Rudolph: *Education and Politics in India*, Harvard University Press, Cambridge, 1972.

Sateswari Saxena: *Education Planning in India: A Study in Approach and Methodology*, Sterling Publishers, New Delhi, 1974.

Singh, M.K.: *Teaching of English*, International Publishing House, Meerut, 1998.

Srivastava, B.D.: *Structural Approach to the Techniques of English*, Ram Parshad and Sons, Agra, 1966.

Srivastava, R.P.: *The Teaching of Reading*, Bahari Publishers, New Delhi, 1979.

Tiwari, D.D.: *Education at the Cross Roads*, Chugh Publications, Allahabad, 1975.

Thomas, F. Station: *Dynamics of Adjustment*, MacMillan Co., New York, 1953.

INDEX

A

Adult Education, 122.
Audio-Visual Aids, 93, 104, 116, 117, 118, 119, 120, 121, 122.
Audio-Visual Materials, 94, 95, 119.

B

Basic Education, 259.
Books, 7, 14, 23, 51, 94, 117, 129, 137, 138, 141, 155, 156, 157, 158, 159, 160, 161, 162, 163, 164, 166, 167, 168, 169, 170, 171, 172, 174, 175, 176, 177, 178, 179, 180, 181, 182, 183, 184, 185, 186, 187, 189, 190, 191, 192, 193, 194, 195, 200, 204, 207, 209, 212, 213, 215, 216, 217, 218, 221, 222, 240, 252.

C

CBSE, 249, 257.
Central Board of Education (, 257.
Computer, 94, 95, 117, 158.

D

Database Programmes, 159.

E

Education, 8, 15, 17, 59, 60, 72, 73, 77, 78, 79, 80, 81, 82, 93, 107, 112, 114, 117, 118, 119, 122, 135, 136, 137, 138, 141, 144, 148, 149, 150, 151, 154, 158, 159, 160, 161, 164, 165, 172, 173, 174, 175, 184, 185, 188, 190, 191, 192, 212, 231, 232, 235, 237, 238, 241, 242, 244, 247, 250, 257, 258, 259, 260.
Education Commission, 81, 107, 137, 138, 144, 151, 237.
Educational Policy, 141.

Educational Technology, 117, 167.
English, 4, 5, 6, 8, 10, 12, 15, 16, 17, 18, 22, 27, 37, 38, 39, 46, 48, 49, 50, 51, 52, 53, 54, 55, 56, 57, 58, 59, 93, 113, 123, 125, 126, 127, 128, 130, 131, 132, 133, 135, 136, 137, 138, 139, 140, 141, 142, 143, 144, 145, 146, 147, 148, 149, 150, 151, 152, 157, 160, 170, 198, 200, 201, 205, 206, 207, 215, 219, 220, 221, 225, 227, 228, 229, 233.
English Language, 125, 139, 140, 141, 142, 143, 144, 146, 147, 148, 150, 198, 205, 206, 228, 229.
English Teaching, 27, 123.
Examinations, 128, 130, 197, 229, 232, 233, 235.

F

Foreign Language, 13, 14, 46, 47, 50, 56, 124, 125, 135, 146, 215, 219, 220, 221.
Fundamental Principle, 56.

G

Gandhi, 137, 140, 142, 148, 179, 259.
Government, 93, 102, 136, 149, 150, 151, 155, 156, 160, 163, 165, 169, 172, 173, 180, 181, 182, 183, 184, 185, 186, 190, 191, 192, 193, 194, 195.
Government Policy, 192.
Grammar, 8, 9, 14, 22, 27, 33, 39, 41, 47, 50, 53, 56, 57, 58, 128, 134, 191, 215.
Guidance, 8, 25, 78, 159, 193, 204, 209, 234.

H

Higher Education, 138, 141, 150.
Hindi, 4, 56, 93, 125, 126, 127, 135, 136, 140, 149, 150, 151, 152, 227.

I

Indian Language, 151, 152.
Indian Students, 136, 143, 148.
Institutions, 114, 116, 155, 158, 197, 230, 231, 233.
International Language, 139, 152.

K

Kothari Commission, 78, 119, 259.
Kothari Education Commission, 137, 138, 151.

L

Language, 8, 9, 10, 11, 12, 13, 14, 15, 28, 29, 33, 34, 36, 37, 38, 39, 41, 42, 43, 44, 45, 46, 47, 48, 49, 50, 52, 54, 55, 56, 57, 58, 78, 83, 93, 94, 95, 106, 112, 124, 125, 126, 127, 128, 130, 131, 134, 135, 136, 137, 138, 139, 140, 141, 142,

143, 144, 145, 146, 147, 148, 149, 150, 151, 152, 157, 165, 166, 167, 170, 178, 179, 195, 197, 198, 201, 202, 203, 205, 206, 208, 209, 210, 211, 212, 213, 214, 215, 217, 219, 220, 221, 222, 224, 225, 227, 228, 229, 233, 235.
Learning, 2, 3, 4, 6, 7, 8, 9, 10, 12, 13, 14, 16, 18, 19, 20, 21, 22, 23, 24, 25, 45, 46, 49, 50, 52, 54, 55, 56, 57, 58, 70, 75, 78, 79, 80, 83, 84, 85, 86, 87, 89, 91, 92, 95, 104, 105, 111, 112, 113, 114, 115, 116, 117, 118, 119, 120, 121, 122, 123, 124, 125, 127, 128, 130, 131, 132, 133, 138, 139, 146, 147, 150, 154, 159, 161, 162, 166, 167, 169, 172, 175, 177, 182, 186, 189, 197, 198, 201, 203, 204, 208, 211, 212, 213, 214, 215, 219, 220, 224, 227, 228, 229, 233, 234, 237, 238, 240, 243, 246, 249, 256, 257, 258, 259.
Learning Programme, 139.
Libraries, 93, 129, 175, 176, 177, 178, 179, 186, 189.
Literacy, 36, 161, 177, 178, 182, 189, 239, 253, 254.

M

Mahatma Gandhi, 142, 148, 259.
Ministry of Education, 158, 168, 175, 177, 184, 185, 190, 192, 194.

N

National Education Conference, 259, 260.
National Language, 139, 149, 150, 167.
National Policy, 119, 149.
NCERT, 78, 129.

P

Patel Committee, 259, 260.
Philosophy, 47, 56, 59, 191, 259.
Primary School, 80, 190, 191, 241.
Printing Press, 189.
Psychological Principles, 2, 21, 71.

R

Regional Language, 149, 150, 151, 152.
Rural Development, 179.

S

Sanskrit, 38, 151.
Scholarship, 144.
School Library, 175, 176.
Science and Technology, 77, 79, 83, 107, 133, 142, 143, 149, 152.
Secondary Education, 107, 244.
Socially Useful Productive Work, 237, 259.
Students, 1, 2, 3, 4, 5, 6, 7, 8, 9, 10, 11, 12, 14, 16, 17, 18, 19, 20, 21, 22, 23, 24, 25, 45, 48,

49, 50, 53, 55, 57, 58, 60, 67, 68, 70, 75, 76, 77, 81, 83, 85, 90, 91, 92, 93, 96, 97, 99, 100, 101, 105, 106, 107, 108, 109, 110, 113, 114, 115, 119, 120, 121, 122, 127, 128, 130, 131, 136, 137, 143, 144, 148, 151, 152, 162, 164, 165, 174, 184, 191, 197, 198, 200, 201, 203, 204, 205, 207, 208, 209, 210, 212, 213, 214, 215, 216, 217, 218, 219, 220, 221, 222, 223, 224, 225, 226, 227, 228, 229, 230, 231, 232, 235, 238, 239, 240, 241, 242, 243, 244, 245, 246, 248, 249, 250, 252, 253, 255, 256, 257, 258.

T

Teacher Training, 231, 239.
Teaching English, 4, 6, 15, 18, 22, 46, 48, 49, 50, 53, 54, 55, 56, 57, 59, 127, 128, 131, 132, 136, 147, 149, 233.
Technology, 77, 79, 80, 83, 107, 112, 114, 116, 117, 133, 141, 142, 143, 144, 145, 149, 152, 167, 237.
Textbook, 7, 79, 84, 85, 117, 128, 153, 155, 156, 157, 158, 159, 160, 161, 163, 165, 167, 168, 169, 170, 171, 172, 174, 177, 180, 182, 183, 184, 185, 186, 187, 189, 190, 191, 192, 193, 194, 195, 215.
TV Programmes, 17.

U

UNESCO, 167, 168, 177.
United States Agency for International Aid, 192.
University, 71, 81, 123, 144.

V

Vocabulary, 9, 10, 13, 46, 48, 50, 53, 133, 214, 240, 247.
Vocational Education, 258.

Y

Yearbook, 158.

❑❑❑